The Indian Rivers Krishna, Godavari Saga

THE THOUGHT

A JOURNEY OF SEVEN GENERATIONS

Translated By Dr.Raghu Ram Ph.D

Author

SUDHEER REDDY PAMIREDDY

The Thought, A Journey of Seven Generations.

First Edition: July 2021

ISBN Paperback   : 978-93-5473-936-1

ISBN e-book   : 978-93-5493-096-6

Copyright © Sudheer Reddy Pamireddy

Cover Design, Pictures: K.VenuMadhav

Published By

Kasturi Vijayam,

3-50, Main Road,

Dokiparru Village -521322

Krishna Dist, Andhra Pradesh, India.

Online/E-book

www.kasturivijayam.com,

www.Amazon.com

play.google.com

Translated By

Dr. Raghu Ram Ph.D

Proof Read By

Padmaja Pamireddy MCA, M.Tech

Whatsapp : +91 95150 54998.

Email: kasturivijayam@gmail.com

This research book is dedicated
to our Grandmother, the late Pamireddy Kasturi,
&
our Grandfather, the late Shri Pamireddy Subbareddy.

Sudheer Reddy Pamireddy – Padmaja

ACKNOWLEDGMENTS

For everyone, who made this book presentable,
Firstly, I thank my wife, Padmaja Pamireddy MCA, M.Tech
&
Dr. Raghuram Ph.D

Secondly, I thank Krishna Rao Boinapalli & Geetha Sunil
for contributing to proofreading this book.

The main reason I am writing this book because of my son, Rama Linga
Reddy Pamireddy & Daughter, Tejo Samiksha Pamireddy, who would
ask me to tell them a story every night.

TABLE OF CONTENTS

INTRODUCTION

The footsteps of 18th-century humans brought about many monumental changes in world history. Those were the days the Whites were assuming that whichever land they reached through the sea route belonged to them. The incidents of that century changed the evolutionary course of India too. With an army of fifty thousand, just five thousand British officers ruled over this land of thirty crore population for two hundred years! The people who came here as merchants grew into much more than that. This is a historical fact. Every generation must-read history to know about these facts.

The wealthiest area of India, the Bengal region, fell to the British first and faced famines eventually, with lakhs getting buried within no time. After plundering the wealth of many sons of this soil, the British turned arrogant beyond measure and brought about two world wars upon this world, causing irreparable damage. The impact of these world wars on India, too, is very deep and must be remembered.

The Vande Mataram Movement gave rise to four decades of relentless agitations of different kinds, leading up to the country's eventual independence. These tumultuous times have also brought upon several changes in the lives of the common men of India, leaving lasting changes that are depicted here. The life of the common man can be described as peaceful yet filled with lots of hardships.

How did "Kanya Shulkam" come about at all in the backdrop of movements in favor of usage of the language of the common man as opposed to archaic, bookish language, and rose to be given the status of a school textbook? The time taken for this change to come about was twenty-five years. Though the victory belonged to the followers of archaic language in this war, the popular writers took up the mantle of the common man's language in their works. We must be acquainted with the way how schools started teaching in local languages and also how the working-class castes grouped separately and fought for their share in the job market. Accountancy and land record maintenance jobs that were limited to certain castes settled into "Karanam" caste hegemony and became synonymous with corrupt, illegal practices. The sayings like "Never trust a bookkeeper" grew from such conditions. These classes also misrepresented the history of the country and wrote it surrounding the migrant rulers.

The readers should decide for themselves which of the incidents described in this book are topical or not. The person born in very common surroundings also grew to reach unimaginable heights, as is shown in this book. Mentioning those remarkable journeys here again would be equal to catching mountains in mirrors.

This book describes the lives of ordinary farmers from two hundred years ago, their lifestyles, cultural practices, their experiences, the various changes that came about in their lives, the reasons behind them in an easy narrative. The practice of combined farming, judicious use of water resources, the structure of large, combined families, the beliefs and bonds that kept them together are all described in this book. The crookedness of the ruling classes, political leaders, and the simple-minded nature of these agrarian societies also takes a major place in this book.

The knowledge of these things could become a guide to future generations. Past to present and present to future are the best foundations. Writing about the past in the form of history and reading about it gives the future generations the best course forward. Writing of history to appease the victors or to sing about them would submerge the world in deep ignorance, I believe. The history books that present the angle of the victors only would be bereft of any human angle. The belief that readers would prefer books written in such a manner is not true at all. Against usual traditions, this book is written taking the path of the common man's social commentary. This book is written with no bias for any particular class or caste.

History is a mix of polity, civics, economics, culture, and psychology. The way to all these sciences is also through history only. That is why the ruling classes make sure that histories are written favoring their angle. If we search histories seriously enough, we can learn that rulers plan their administration carefully, watching the flow of thought of the society and the twists and turns in that stream.

Man's true happiness comes from within. History is the compilation of the thinking of society. Studying history gives people the knowledge of their roots. It is a way of knowing the structure and contours of their society's structure. I am hopeful that readers of this book would study and debate all issues discussed in this book. Let's proceed!

Sudheer Reddy Pamireddy

FOREWORDS

Truly... Another "Seven Generations"!

Professor Rachapalem Chandra Shekhar Reddy

Indian classical and Modern Literature Critic

Anantapuram

Andhra Pradesh

India.

"Internal discipline is the only way to greatness. When you affix yourself to a great task, it will bring out your innermost hidden strengths." (The Thought – A Journey of Seven Generations – Page: 175)

After reading the book "The Thought – A Journey of Seven Generations", written by Sudheer Reddy Pamireddy, I felt most surprised with and to the writer's range of thought and zeal for investigation attracted. "The Thought" is a book that mixes history with literature. At the same time, it is also a book that mixes research with a lot of persuasions. The writer did not simply limit himself to writing whatever he knew about his clan, his village, or the region; but consulted lots of important books to gather material for the history he was penning down. This zeal is what attracts us to this writing. The writer used a methodology of constructing philosophical theory around sociological happenings, incidents and their repercussions before adding his own commentary to them. He did not simply fill his book with an ocean of information but interpreted that information with historical, philosophical thought, which gave the book the maturity it carries.

For a cursory glance, the book seems to describe the lives of the acquaintances of the writer from the Pakanadu region - who made a name for themselves, who spread to far off regions, who got into money, who among them were the hard workers and who were not, etc. but the book is not just about this. It carries many propositions too. The writer's comments on the history, the way it progressed really stand out. The writer really succeeded in picking up the various reasons behind the economic, social, political, and cultural changes in the Telugu region of India from the 18th century onwards.

Mr. Sudheer Reddy has strong likes and dislikes. He presents his likes so eloquently, and is equally tough in declaring his dislikes. Persons who might agree with his opinions also might feel that he is being injudicious in his dislikes. Soon, they would understand that the writer is equanimous and has conveyed right and wrong truthfully, without mincing words.

The book is the result of a search to find what happened to the Pamireddy families that migrated from the Pakanadu region of Rayalaseema to the Coastal belt due to the pressure from migrant rulers. That's why the book is compared to Alex Haley's "Roots", and Karanam Balasubramanyam's "Boya Kottamulu Pandrendu" by Mr.Vishesh. The book describes the history of seven generations of Pamireddy family members and the history of the several regions associated with them. Sudheer Reddy studied Mackenzie's "Kaifiyat", and several other books to gather information for this. Mr. Akella Raghavendra mentions just this and calls the book a Kaifiyat.

The book starts with the twisted policy adopted by the migrant rulers after they settled to rule India and concludes with the description of the growth of a few Pamireddy family members and relatives in the industrial scenario of the present day.

After reading about how Colonel Colin Mackenzie, with the help of few local administrators, suppressed the Chenchu's living in the Sri Shailam Forest region, we are compelled to reconsider our opinion about Mackenzie. The discrepancy in the number of temples claimed to be constructed by Vasireddy Venkatadri Naidu generally in history is also pointed out by the author. The true origin of the Kohinoor diamond is also claimed to be the Kolluru village of the Gunturu district by the author. He further describes the hardships faced by the locals who supported Mackenzie. He reveals that it was Mackenzie and Munro's design to shift expert agriculture farmers from Pakanadu to Krishna and Godavari districts.

The story really begins at this juncture,going ahead, describes the process and specific settlements of these farmers in coastal villages. The Journey of the Pamireddy Lingareddy family, how they relentlessly struggled to keep up their expertise in the various fields they entered, is brought to life in the further stages. The story of these farmers who fused their lives with the soil to grow some grains and how they grew to become the founders of companies like Megha Engineering becomes the main narrative of the book.

We have to specially note Sudheer Reddy's viewpoint with regard to sharing water resources. "The distribution of water should not be on the basis of linguistic states. What is the link between water and language? The criteria should only look into places with water availability and those without. This is a humanist approach" (Page: 196).

The rulers should respect such opinions. Sudheer Reddy also says that if the Sarkar Districts grow a big heart, then Rayala Seema would become an ever-green region (Page: 198). The writer also raises the issue of tribals displaced by the Polavaram project (Page: 196). He also described the socially responsible conduct of the Pamireddy families after they grew affluent (Page: 177).

The opportunism of Zamindars described in this book is really an eye-opener to many (Page: 67). The history of Dokiparru village is recorded quite realistically in this book. This region was filled with freedom fighters. While explaining the differences between Gandhi and Ambedkar, the writer goes on to explain how they were exploited by the migrant rulers. He did not hesitate from pointing out the autocratic nature in Gandhi, who was beyond reproach generally. The writer also explained the relation between the politics of those days and cinema in a manner of documentation.

Everybody aged 18 and above are eligible to vote presently, but the same privilege was accorded only to those who had an amount of 100 rupees with them in 1937. This revelation by the writer points out the social advances our society has made. Conscious citizens used the ballot papers to vent their ire even in those days, reminds the book (Page: 85). The freedom struggle, bifurcation of the country, birth of united India, Telangana Armed Struggle, Rajaji's politics, the birth of Andhra, Andhra Pradesh, and several other historical events are also described by Sudheer Reddy within the narrative. The role played by their village and clan in all these incidents is beautifully presented by Sudheer Reddy.

Though Sudheer Reddy displays traits of romanticism, his opinions are highly exalted. Some of his comments are sure to attract.

"For any task, awareness of duty, resolve, and understanding of capacity is needed."

"River water doesn't run around the feet of politicians like their pet dogs."

This book shows that Sudheer Reddy has studied ancient and modern literature in depth. This study is used expertly in this book from time to time.

History, politics, economics, cultural details, human relations are expertly combined in this book by Sudheer Reddy, and he should be commended for this effort. This book truly gives a feeling of touring all the Telugu land while reading. Truly, this book is another "Seven Generations!"

"Rainfall, lakes, groundwater, river flows, etc., all should be taken into consideration when distributing a natural resource like water among humans (Page: 198)".

Dasu Kesava Rao

Independent Journalist,
Former Deputy Editor & Chief of Bureau,
The Hindu, Hyderabad, Telangana, India
Mobile: 8886277707
dasukesavarao@gmail.com

History is supposed to be an objective and unbiased account of events of the past. However, it is more often misinterpreted or even distorted to suit the rulers and the times. A case in point is the depiction of the Mughal and the British rulers. Modern history is also not without aberrations, such as attempts to glorify some leaders and marginalize others for their contribution to the freedom struggle.

Recent times have seen attempts to correct these aberrations and put things in proper perspective. One such attempt is '*The Thought, A Journey of Seven Generations*', authored by a young researcher, Dr. Pamireddy Sudheer Reddy.

'*The Thought*' is the social, economic, and cultural history of the Pakanaadu region of Andhra Pradesh from the 19th century on, interwoven with the family history of Pakanaadu Reddys to which the author belongs. Usually, a book of this kind ought to interest only the concerned community, making it staid and boring for others. Yet Dr. Sudheer Reddy illuminates the book with a sympathetic portrayal of ordinary people's lives – their joys and sorrows, hopes and despair, even their eating and dressing style – against the backdrop of the freedom struggle.

Colonial manuals, manuscripts, and administrative procedures evolved during the period of administrators like Colin McKenzie and Thomas Munro have become benchmark for researchers and a virtual gospel for bureaucrats who swear by these names. The author, however, has other views. Be it McKenzie or Munro, and he contends that they arrived in India with a clear agenda to impose their own education system and cart away India's material and spiritual wealth with the cooperation of native collaborators. The good word is, however, reserved for Arthur Cotton and C.P. Brown.

In his assessment of the stalwarts of the nationalist movement, he has not spared even Mahatma Gandhi or C. Rajagopalachari for their foibles. Gandhi was sometimes autocratic and intolerant of opinions contrary to his own. When Subhash Chandra Bose defeated his nominee B. Pattabhi Sitaramayya in the Congress party elections, Gandhi viewed it as his own defeat. Again, he could not take it kindly to the victory of Tanguturi Prakasam over his nominee C. Rajagopalachari as the choice for the post of the Prime Minister of the Madras Presidency in 1946. He accused Prakasam of misusing donations collected for the party and that on this score, and he was not eligible to contest. Ambedkar also had a similar experience with Gandhi for differing with him. Rajaji was a wily politician who missed no opportunity to humiliate Telugu and their culture in the undivided Madras Presidency. He described the Telugu people as 'Aarambha Soorulu' capable of beginning things with a bang yet petering out quickly.

In the evaluation of successive chief ministers of Andhra Pradesh, the author appears to falter in being objective and impartial. His assertion that NT Rama Rao was reinstated as the Chief Minister after apologizing to Indira Gandhi sounds strange. NTR owed this to the whole-hearted support of the masses, the media, and the non-Congress opposition parties, a fact acknowledged all around.

Alongside the history of Pakanaadu, Paakanaati Reddys, and the freedom movement, there runs an equally interesting story of the growth of irrigation from the times of Arthur Cotton to the present.

The narration runs like a box office cinema script laced with intrigue, treachery, violence, and revenge. The book opens with a chapter on the Chenchus, the innocent and age-old inhabitants of the Nallamala forests who paid a heavy price for defying the might of McKenzie and Raja Vasireddy Venkatadri Naidu of Chinthapalli Samsthanam. No fewer than 500 Chenchus were lured out of the safety of their forest and butchered. It was a dark, shameful chapter in history that went unnoticed. Call it retribution or a curse of the Chenchu widows, and the Rajah had no peace despite all the wealth and power. He was killed by remorse. It was said that to atone for his sins, the Raja had constructed 108 temples and showered gold on Brahmin priests. The Vasireddy family history put the figure at 108 temples and the McKenzie kaifiyat at 180. Despite the fact that the author maintains that Vasireddy Raja had built only nine temples. He regrets that the media continue to believe exaggerated versions and persist in propagating them. 'Is this not a distortion of history? He wonders. The Chenchus were branded as Pindaris, witch-hunted and killed.

Dokiparru village in the erstwhile Char Mahal samsthanam of Krishna district figures prominently in the account of the freedom struggle and literacy promotion. Dokiparru elders requested Dasu Sreeramulu, a teacher in the neighbouring Kowtharam, to set up a school for their children. Sreeramulu served the village with utmost dedication, his pupils representing all castes. When he moved to Machilipatnam to begin a legal career, the grateful Dokiparru people showered him with gold flowers (Swarna Pushpam) and gifted him a palanquin on which he was carried around the village. Mahakavi Sreeramulu was a multi-splendoured genius who was hailed as Abhinava Srinadha. Devi Bhagavatham in Telugu is his magnum opus.

Dokiparru elders broke down the practice that required people to turn over money received at a party or marriage functions ('Pelli Chadivimpulu') to the libraries. The cost of ignorance is well brought out by the experience of a widow who gave away bundles of currency notes to a vendor thinking it was waste paper. The woman did not know what she threw away was the hard-earned money her husband had left for her.

The book deals at length with the impact of Bandaru Uppena or the catastrophic tidal wave (1864) and equally tragic famine of 1832-33, known as Nandana (name of the year) karuvu.

The author enlivens the book with some interesting yet lesser-known nuggets from the past. Sample these. Thomas Munro, Governor of Madras at the time, was passing through the Nallamala forests when he spotted a shimmering gold chain hanging from a tamarind tree. An elderly Chenchu told him it was visible only to those at the doorstep of death. Fear of death has haunted Munro ever since, and he died of cholera in Pattikonda in Kurnool district. Munro was known for the merciless quelling of the Palegar rebellion.

People living along the Godavari believed it was sacrilege to block the river by building a dam or an anicut. However, things changed after Arthur Cotton built the barrage across the mighty river. In the early 30s, people travelling by rickshaw were teased and heckled by children.

How did Arthur Cotton get his job? He and two others were shortlisted for the final interview. They were lodged for the night in a room with well-furnished beds. Cotton noticed that the cot did not rest properly and made a squeaking noise. He got up to inquire and noticed a coin placed under one of the legs. 'How did the night go? The interviewers asked. While the two men said they had a good sleep,

Cotton said he was troubled by the coin. Cotton was selected because he had a natural curiosity, which the other two lacked, although a coin was placed under their cot too.

The visit of the Simon Commission evoked nationwide protests. When Simon halted at Bezawada railway station, Ayyadevara Kaleswara Rao, municipal chairman, sent a letter through colleague Ramireddy Subba Reddy, disguised as a messenger, demanding that Simon 'go back. Simon seethed with anger, still could not vent it on a mere messenger!

The book is a rich mine of information, complete with photos and sketches for the general reader and the inquisitive young people interested in culture and history.

Prof.Dr Ravi Kiran Vatrapu

Loretta Rogers Chair & Professor at Ted Rogers School of Management - Ryerson University

Canada

This is an ambitious book that seeks to narrate the historical origins and accomplishments of select families from a set of close-knit villages spread across the Krishna and Godavari river deltas in the state of Andhra Pradesh, India. It is a commendable effort given that this is not only the debut book but also that the author is not a trained cultural historian. This also means that the book reads as a collection of narratives spanning the historical time from the first establishment of the East India Company on the Southern shores of India in Machilipatnam in 1611 to the present times. Despite its sometimes uneven and disjointed feel, the book achieves its primary task of narrating the story of migration, settlement, and achievements of a community. I found it remarkable that, unlike other diasporas, there seems to little to no engagement with the communities or lands from emigration. Again, in this era of globalization of capital and the global migrations of people seeking economic opportunities and/or safe-havens, the book also tells a tale of how aspirations, assimilation, and acculturation mix at the individual and collective levels in displaced communities. In the end, the book is also a celebration of a selection of successful people within the community. In that sense, the book is an acknowledgement of their contributions to not only their immediate social networks but to society at large.

Lastly, unlike other parts of the world, India in general and South India in particular has astonishingly low engagement with the historical record in public life. It seems like the general attitude is that history is something that happened to others in other places, and the past is indeed a strange country lost in the concerns of the present. I hope that this book spurs the creative energies of intellectually curious individuals in the region and beyond and result in a plethora of voices telling their own tales of movement and betterment.

✳✳✳

Associate Professor Dr. Subramaniam Sri Ramalu
FCMI Director, Postgraduate Studies, Unit College of Business
Universiti Utara Malaysia
Malaysia

"Each new generation is reared by its predecessor; the latter must therefore improve in order to improve its successor. The movement is circular." *-- Emile Durkheim.*

'The Thought, A Journey of Seven Generations' thoughtfully describes the hardships of the country, state, and village conflicts that took place over the course of four eras and seven generations of evolution. This book is based on biographies. As I read this book, the main thing that struck me was the sequence of human evolution, culture, and family values that change over period.

Our minds get very excited when we read the life experiences of seven generations of Pakanati. The author walks through the symbiotic relationships between the individual and how the society around him was developed. It shows the social changes in the lifestyle over time and says that the footprints of the older generations are the guides for the next generations.

It is interesting to note that water has been a central point of the discussion in this book. As we know, water is essential in human life. The book narrates how the water problem is transmitted from one generation to another and how it solves problems with the evolving human thought process from generation to generation. It introduces the living conditions of the ordinary people around the water, the needs of the peasant families associated with water, the political evolution, the modern changes in the field of irrigation, and the business principles combined in the hydrology projects. It is also commendable to show literary evidence for each event that took place.

Broadly speaking, the book has enlightened the Journey and experiences of seven generations of Telugu people's economic and cultural conditions, understanding of nature, association with agriculture, hopes, aspirations, struggles, shortcomings, compromises, and exaltations about the country.

As a Telegu descent who were born in Malaysia, I follow the development closely in India, particularly in states where the majority of Telegu people are residing. As a senior faculty who is specialising in organizational behaviour and cross-cultural studies, I am honoured to read the book and give my foreword. Thank you to Mr. Pamireddy Sudheer Reddy, our doctoral student at Universiti Utara Malaysia, for this opportunity.

The visionary of Pakanati's and their contribution to the Motherland

Sesha Sai Praneeth Kanumuri,M.Tech
Research Assistant,
Pierre and Curie University, France.

"We are just stars in our family's constellation."

--Stephen Robert Kuta.

I am one of the stars in the family tree of Kanumuri Ganapathi Reddy (First Generation). It is my privilege to express my perspective on the book "The Thought – A Journey of Seven Generations." The author Pamireddy Sudheer Reddy is a distinct relative, and when we first discussed his thoughts on my seven-generation history, I felt so stunning the way he investigated the past, gathered the evidence, and continuing his groundwork. It is nearly an excellent research ability for an individual person to have such patience in searching for truth.

To know the history, we have to listen and go inside to what people are saying. During his writings, the author successfully followed the statement and hasn't judged anyone, though he questioned the situations that happened in the past. The readers will be emphasized by the efforts and blood spilled of our ancestors, which leads to forming an independent India. In the freedom, Gandhiji had visited southern states six times. In every visit, the ordinary person's contribution was also beyond their power; donation of gold and money. There is less information in Indian history about the southern warriors. This book has summarized this data and tries to explain the background scenarios. Very few writers are expressing their thoughts unbiasedly, and I feel he is one of them.

Coming to the book's main objective, to connect the filled gaps in the history of Andhra Pradesh and the role of the Pakanati in those movements. I felt proud to know the facts that my ancestors are also part of freedom struggles. On the other part, I also witnessed the British unethical divide and rule policies, and I was always wondering how do

Indians fall into the trap of the British empire, the author illustrated with a lot of schemas, particularly the tribal people suffered and lost their source of faith and surrendered as slaves for their livelihood.

Further in investing the facts and truth that lies underneath the village Dokiparru, the Megha family's tree contributes in many aspects. Starting from his great grandfathers, the service they have given to the village is unconditional. "Even Roma can't be built in a day", in the same slogan, great ancestries from our families constructed the village Dokiparru from the 19th century until today. Our two families are like bulls that help to plough the irrigation land and ruling the village ever since the formation of panchayathis. Firstly, they started with digging lakes, canals, establishing government schools, and now, under the direction of the MEIL organization, the village has everything. From transportation to running water, electricity to employment opportunities. During the pandemic of COVID-19, they concentrated on hospital facilities, Oxygen availability, and the distribution of vaccines for Dokiparriens. And I would like to compare the author's attitude from the quotes of Henry S.F. Cooper **"A man who overthinks about his ancestors is like a potato – the best part of him is underground."**

Especially, I thank the author for his efforts to collect the rightful info and to scrutinize. The author's wife, Padmaja's support, is remarkable. The author usually says to me, "If you don't know history, you don't know anything. You are a leaf that doesn't know it is part of a tree." So, this might be the reason he rooted his family tree in this writing. I am thankful to the author for giving me this opportunity to express my point of view. On behalf of my beloved father, Kanumuri Gopala Krishna Reddy (late), I would like to thank him, who endeavours to collect the family member details and cross-check the provided information.

SOUND OF SILENCE

The East India Company established a factory at Masulipatnam (present Machilipatnam) in the year 1611. The deep-rooted distrust and discord among the innumerable kingdoms/ Samsthanas in India and the British's desire to conquer India led to form three provinces: Madras, Bombay, and Bengal Presidencies in 1640, 1687, and 1690 years respectively. Finally, British India has been formed in over 80 years. The States of Andhra, Tamil Nadu, Kerala, Orissa, Karnataka, and Lakshadweep were part of the Madras Presidency. After pushing out the French from the Sarkar districts in 1759, the Company reorganized the area with three administrative centres in Ganjam, Vishakhapatnam, and Machilipatnam. The usurping and expansion of the British rule continued unabated with the sole objective of plundering the wealth of all Indian Samsthanas. India was just like a cash cow, and the British wanted to milk to the last drop.

The Krishna River Bay Area – Chenchus

The Eastern Ghat range of India is home to the Nallamala forest spread in the five districts of – Mahabub Nagar, Kurnool, Prakasham, Guntur, Kadapa, and part of Nalgonda districts in present Andhra and the Telangana States. Nallamala is home to abundant nature and incredible flora and fauna. Layover a region of 800 square kilometres, the forest is a true and complete witness of nature. The forest also has a serenity that is perfect for philosophical and spiritual contemplation. The Shri Shaila Kshetra, situated amidst the rocky terrain, is the sacred abode of God Shree Mallikarjuna. It is one of the twelve sacred Jyotirlingas that the entire Hindus venerate. Shri Bhramarambika also one of the centres of the eighteen most powerful Shakti Peethas.

The natives of this forest, the Chenchus, are among the oldest tribes on earth. Their primary God is dearly referred to by them as Shree Shaila Lingamayya. When Chatrapati Shivaji visited Shri Shailam, the Chenchus were the main priests at the temple, as per history. These Chenchus are like ascetics/yogi's finely updated to the movement of the

time itself and lead their lives as per the changes in the Universal Constellation. They can even understand the changes in the twittering of the birds and guess the harm is coming their way. This minute knowledge and understanding of nature give them the ability to live as one with all the animals, birds, and insects of this forest. The burrows, tunnels, and caves of these hills are their home. Their colonies are called "Penta". Each "Penta" will have a Chenchu leader. Their huts are generally designed in the shape of a Conch Shell[1]. They prefer living within their community and do not usually mix with other groups.

Famous poet Gurram Jashuva, in his acclaimed long poem "Gabbilam", described them like this:

Wielding the arrow and bow, standing in the middle of the forest;

If you come across these Chenchus, do salute! He might be Lord Shiva himself,

Playing in this disguise as a Bhillu, hunting imaginary pigs;

Giving away offerings to the devotees travelling through this Jungle to the temple

Jashuva – Gabbilam

Palkuriki Somanadha also mentions in his "Panditaradhya Charitra" that these Chenchus act as helpers to the Shiva devotees travelling through these jungles, offering them water and food. Maha Shivaratri is the most auspicious festival for them. They celebrate it with great enthusiasm and spiritual fervour. Their financial transactions are based on the barter system mostly. They never worry about the future and are fully immersed in spending the immediate moment with equanimity.

Colin Mackenzie

Colonel Colin Mackenzie (1754) was born on the island of Lewis of Scotland called Stornoway. His father, Murdoch Mackenzie, was a postmaster there. His mother was Barbara Mackenzie. Colin Mackenzie's first-ever job was as an accountant for a rich man called John Napier. Napier was a history buff and a collector of antiques. His son-in-law, Samuel Johnston, came to India and settled in Telugu land in the town of Madhira as an employee of the East India Company. Napier's daughter, Hester, established friendly relations with the Niyogi Brahmin scholars who belonged to that area.

Colin Mackenzie entered India in 1783 when he was 30 years old. Using Hester's good offices with the Niyogi Brahmins of Madhira, Mackenzie collected historical information on the region's temples.

Later he joined the East India Company Army team during1784-1790 to create the geographical survey maps of the Nellore, Nallamala, and the Erramala hill region (Pakanadu region). Like a wolf offered to be the guard for a troop of goats, Mackenzie joined the survey team without any pay or provisions. He slowly became an integral part of the team and took over the responsibilities of surveying the Guntur region from the East India Company. In 1790 - 93, Mackenzie surveyed the Guntur district and Krishna, Godavari, Vishakhapatnam, and Ganjam regions. He took care to include the histories of local temples of the region, the details of donated lands to the occupational caste groups, histories of villages, regional folk tales, historical anecdotes, beliefs, customs, and religious beliefs in the local history records called "Kaifiyat" [2].

With a specific agenda, he took an interest in gathering the information of the areas on the south side of Krishna River – the Adopted Mandals and Guntur area, where historical records of hidden treasures were mentioned. If the Kaifiyats are observed, we can deduce that he did not focus much on the historical records of the north side of the Krishna River.

Kavali Brothers

Kavali Brothers find a special place in the regional history of the 18th Century. These are five brothers - Naraynappa, Venkata Borrayya, Venkata Lakshmayya, Venkata Ramaswami, and Seetayya; Eluru born Niyogi (six thousand) Brahmins who wrote the history of the 18th Century in many ways. Narayanappa was Mackenzies's "Dubasi". "Dubasi" is a person who is adept at two languages – a translator with expertise in local language and also English. Dubasi is the most important conduit for any White Lord. He will introduce all the important people of the area to the Lord, and all-important Company work is handled through him. For the local people, he becomes the mouthpiece of the Company and the go-to guy for any official communication. Kavali Borrayya learnt English at the age of 14 in Bandaru's Morgan School. In the later years, he became an indispensable hand to Col. Mackenzie[3].

Why Don't These People Understand?

By the time he started surveying the adopted Mandals, Mackenzie had already acquired a good knowledge of India's ancient, eternal history through John Napier. When Borrayya's team dug at Shree Shaila Kshetra's Jagadguru Adi Shankaracharya's Retreat (Mutt) for their survey, they found deep tunnels. When the Chenchu priests knew about this, they feared divine wrath and assumed that these teams are gold-digging thieves hunting for treasures and chased them away from the area. Feeling hurt and humiliated, Borrayya added ten things to the incident and reported it all to Mackenzie.

A typical English egoist, Mackenzie felt it as an insult to the Crown and declared that he would personally come there for the survey, challenging anybody to come and dare to stop him. Perhaps sensing this threat, about 500 Chenchus had gathered at the temple site, protecting it with their bows and arrows. Borrayya was shocked to see such a strong opposition and tried to placate them, saying that the Lordship had come to pay his respects to the Mallikarjuna Swamy. As Christians and men from other religions are forbidden to enter the Temple, Chenchu leader Ramadasu denied Mackenzie entry into the Sanctum Sanctorum. Despite repeated requests, he said that the foreigner could not be permitted inside the temple.

When Mackenzie was informed about this obstruction, he took it as a personal insult. At that moment, his anger had no bounds. He was huffing and puffing. He warned Borrayya to tell the Chenchus not to undermine his power. Borrayya also told him not to test these tribals on an issue of religious piety. He then came up with a plan and arranged for a big mirror inside the sanctum sanctorum, reflecting the image of the main deity onto another mirror placed outside the main temple. Thus, standing outside the Temple, Mackenzie could see God. This way, Borrayya tried to placate both Chenchus, who were fixed on not letting the foreigner enter the temple, and the Lordship, who was adamant that he visit God [4].

It was nothing more than a face-saving exercise for Mackenzie. He was boiling inside with rage over Chenchu leader Ramadasu. He vowed to show him the real grudge and vengefulness of an English man. He turned all red, seething with anger, ploying his revenge with Borrayya. Dubbing Chenchus as robbers and dangerous bandits began with this incident. Thus, in history, a conspiracy was raised against Chenchus.

Mackenzie and Borrayya covered as many places as possible during the survey. When Mackenzie heard about the valuable historical artefacts in the Amaravathi region, he met Chintapalli Samsthana King Raja Venkatadri Nayudu in 1790 [5].

Raja Vasireddi Venkatadri Nayudu

King of the Chintapalli region, Venkatadri Nayudu, was born on 20th April 1761. Nizam King Basalat Jung beheaded his father, Jagganna, after inviting him on the pretext of a meeting at the Capital. Jagganna's wife, Achamma, offered herself on his funeral pyre as was the custom of the day [6]. Thus, Venkatadri became an orphan at the age of 3. Jagganna's elder brother, Ramanna, took Venkatadri under his care, along with the estate of Chintapalli.

Nayudu was known for his adamant behaviour from childhood and for insistence on carrying out whatever came into his head no matter what. That's how, at the age of 17 (The year 1778), he forcefully married Verremamba. When he became major, he took back the rulership of his Chintapalli Samsthana (1783). A daughter was born, whom he named Rajyalakshmi. Soon he usurped his paternal uncle's estate also, which sheltered him when he was an orphan. In the year 1785, he married again for the sake of a son[7]. The second wife's name was Parvati.

Khammam, Nandigama paragana, Kalidindi paragana, Akulamannadu, Inukuduru, Nemali; Gunturu district's Kondaveedu Seema, Vinukonda Seema, Rayapudi, Chamarti, Ketavaram paragana, Ponnuru, Ravela, Konduru villages, Kolluru, Mangalagiri, Nijam Patnam; Raja Mahendra Varam district's Palivela, Nagaram etc were all part of Chintapalli Samsthana. Being adjacent to Nizam State, Chintapalli was geographically well situated. It served well to the British as a strategic area for a military camp.

Harijan soldiers like Veer Singh, Raam Singh, Bhadra Singh, and Bhujanga Raya; Maratha brave men like Kotaji, Sarsoji, Ramoji, etc., served the Chintapalli Army in key positions. As soon as Nayudu usurped the reins of his Uncle's Samsthana, he put his cousins Naganna and Chandramouli in prison [8]. Around that period, Nayudu's other cousin, Muktyala Samsthanas ruler Vasireddy Lakshmipati was discussing with Company authorities to give him control over some parts of Machilipatnam, which he felt were rightfully his. When Nayudu came to know about this, he sent his armies to Muktyala and destroyed the place.

Usurping his Uncle Ramanna's throne, imprisoning his cousins Chandramouli and Naganna, destroying another cousin Lakshmipati's estate, including his Fort, were the acts of Nayudu's early rule. While others called them greed and violence, Nayudu's palace poets wrote songs calling them acts of bravery and daring.

Nayudu's army chief was Bhujanga Raya, who belonged to the Madiga caste. He was very close to Nayudu. He left no stone unturned in getting the desires of his King fulfilled. Folk tales say that Bhujanga married women from five different sects[9], but with his Muslim wife, he had most children. Another important chieftain was Maratha soldier Ramoji. He was known as an expert in psychological warfare. As the in-charge of Capital's security, he would bring all the important news that is heard in the deepest corners of the kingdom to Nayudu[10].

The Bloodcurdling wails of Chenchus

Borrayya schemed in many ways to satisfy Mackenzie's acrimony with the Chenchus. He wanted to use Nayudu as a chief weapon against the simple-minded tribals as part of those schemes. The British were always looking for ways to enter into the affairs of the rich Samsthanas like Chintapalli. The family feud between Chintapalli and Nandigama Samsthanas gave them the opportunity they were waiting for. Once Borrayya gained Nayudu's ear, he told him that if he brought the Chenchus down on their knees, he might gain the good grace of the British. Nayudu lapped up the suggestion immediately and wrote a letter, dated 25.09.1791, to the Company for permission to capture and bring the thieving Chenchus to justice. The Company, too, acquiesced to the request on the same day and released necessary permissions and sent an army contingent under the leadership of Major Burr to assist [11].

On 11.11.1791, Venkatadri Nayudu, with his Maratha warriors and Company Army team, attacked the Chenchu villages. Because it was the hilly forest area of Nallamala, their stronghold, the Chenchus retaliated with surprise guerilla attacks from behind the hillocks and big trees. With that war, the British realized that they couldn't subjugate the Chenchus in a straight, fair war. They decided to try proxy war.

The region of the war with Chenchus fell under the Nizam rule. After the war, Nayudu declared that he has successfully vanquished Chenchu leader Ram Nayak and the Chenchu village "Kammala Cheruvu" is now under his rule. All Nayudu could manage was killing a Chenchu leader named Chinnu Papayya [12]. So as not to fall on the wrong side with the Nizam, Venkatadri Nayudu went to Golkonda, stayed there for a few days, paid One Lakh Pagoda's (Four Lakhs

Rupees) to Nizam, and got a declaration of being awarded Mannem Sulthan title from Nizam and also Madhira, Kumbham Mettu areas as gifts from him. It is all recorded in the book "Venkatadreendra Charitra" [13].

There were 551 villages in the Chintapalli Samsthana. The tax collection was the responsibility of the Karanams. Each Karanam had about 15 villages under him, with 35 Karanams working for the Samsthana [14]. The Company had doubts regarding the tax collection reports that were being submitted to them. They ordered Nayudu to come before them for an inspection at Machilipatnam in a letter dated 19.11.1791. This was a usual pressure tactic of the British to get their demands met by the Samsthana rulers. On the other side, the Muktyala Samsthana ruler Lakshmipathi negotiated with the British to hand him over the Chintapalli estate for double payment of taxes [15]. The British asked Nayudu for this increased amount of tax directly, raising the number to Rs.7,66,215 Peshkash [16].

The Venkata Giri Samsthanam had 800 villages under it. The Chintapalli Samsthanam had 551 villages. When Venkata Giri was paying a tax of Rs.3,77,085 Peshkash to the Company, Venkatadri Nayudu's Chintapalli was ordered a tax of Rs.7,66,215 Peshkash. Thus despite Nayudu was trying to help the British against the Chenchus, he was being forced to pay more tax. This was a typical example of a British double-edged sword dealing with the Indian Samsthanas.

As these Samsthanas were paying such heavy taxes to the British, they felt free to deal with the public and peasants under their rule in the harshest manner. As Nayudu failed to impress the British in their scheme against the Chenchus the first time, he thought of an extreme step this time. It was the year 1793, and he entrusted the task of crushing the Chenchus to his Prime Minister Papayaradhya[17]. Under his direction, Army Chief Bhujangaraya spent over 16 months in the midst of Chenchus as one among them to gain their trust.

His primary task was to lure as many Chenchus as possible to come to the Chintapalli Palace for some days. He finally convinced Chenchu leader Ramadasu to believe in him and send about 500 Chenchus. He assured them of their well-being, King's protection, and all facilities. The simple-hearted Chenchus believed him as they had already accepted him as one of them and respected him as a leader. So they came in big numbers to experience the King's hospitality.

King Nayudu ordered Minister Papaya and Senadhipati Bhujangaraya to kill all the Chenchus during a single night[18]. Minister

Papaya organized a feast for Chenchus that evening. The Chenchu's favourite Rice laced with Milk was also served on the menu. The Chenchus unwittingly ate their belly full and slept peacefully. In the middle of the night, the soldiers of Bhujangaraya woke them up rudely, shackled their hands and feet, and made them march into the deep forest outside the Fort.

The forest had dense hills that were protruding sharply into the night, with equally long trees piercing the sky. A long walk revealed a big stretch of land that was cleared flat with few tree stumps still declaring their presence there. The sound of the shackles on their hands and feet sounds like the cymbals used in praying Maha Shiva. The shackles on Chenchus were jangling together, sounding as if offering prayer to the Maha Shiva.

The night was still dark as if the Morning Star was hiding in fear. The rivulet flowing beside the cleared space took many curves like a slithering snake and disappeared at a distance. The many swords and sickles that were sharpened and kept ready in several bunches were gleaming in the little light they were catching. The hard breaths of the wives of all the Chenchus were turning sharp and erratic.

Nayudu was sitting in his Royal Palanquin, shifting in his pillows as if eager to watch a great spectacle. Bhujangaraya was feeling heavy in his heart as the memories of his bonding with the Chenchus were coming to him in waves. The soldiers made the Chenchus kneel in several rows. The poor Chenchus were still unaware of what was going to come. They were looking all around with furtive glances, in between staring at the bunches of swords and Bhujanga Raya, who was standing near the King's Palanquin. Bhujangaraya was not returning their stares. It was time.

The Squadron Leaders of the Army received the signal from Nayudu, lifted the sharpened swords, and started cutting the heads from different ends of the rows. Suddenly cries of "Hara Hara Mahadeva", "Om Namah Shivaya" yelling in the quiet night, with sounds of swishing swords in the air and falling heads on the ground. Wives of the Boya's and Chenchus started wailing. Those shrieks would melt even the toughest of the hearts. Some of them were cursing Nayudu. Some were exhorting the Mahadeva to come and save them. Some were flinging the gravel they picked up from the ground into the air, cursing Nayudu and his future generations. Few Chenchus were pleading with Bhujangaraya for intervention.

Within minutes, the number of heads has rolled down. The ground had become muddy with the blood flowing, rendering the movements of the soldiers difficult. The rivulet turned red. Soon, the swords had gone blunt, and the heads were not getting separated smoothly. The soldiers and the swords were replaced. The Mayhem continued. Venkatadri Nayudu, watching it all from the inside of his Palanquin, looked like a possessed man. He was exhorting his soldiers to be swift.

The tired soldiers were finding it hard to even raise their swords. Their clothes were soaked with blood; their hearts were heavy with all the cries and death in the air. They stopped and went near Nayudu's Palanquin and stood motionlessly. Venkatadri Nayudu got down swiftly, his eyes still red, baying for more blood, picked up a sword that was dripping blood all over, and walked towards a Chenchu at one end of a row. "What is your last wish?" commanded the King. The Chenchu, still kneeling and praying with his closed eyes, replied: "Start cutting from the other end, Lord", [19] and went back to his chanting.

The King could not cut the heads of Chenchu leaders Ramadasu, Sri Krishnadasu, Bheemadasu, Venkatadasu and Veeradasu[20]. It was as if the swords were slicing through empty air. The King was baffled. His Minister Papayaraadhya ordered his men to remove the sacred threads with Rudraksha beads from their necks. As soon as those beads were removed, their heads rolled down like the rest of them. The soldiers were pushed again to finish the remaining task. Thus ended the darkest night in the history of Chenchus of the region.

Not expecting the violence and bloodshed of that magnitude, the East India Company, too, tried to wash off its hands, looking at the public outrage. They dumped the whole blame for the Chenchu massacre on Venkatadri Nayudu and ordered several restraining measures. He was put under the custody of Company Battalions to stop him from any further outbursts. Company Officers took over the entire control of Chintapalli Samsthanam on 01.07.1795.

Two battalions were deployed there permanently to oversee security measures. Without bothering Nayudu's consent, on 05.10.1795, the Company officers released Nayudu's cousins Chandramouli and Naganna from Chintapalli prison and declared a monthly stipend for them. Nayudu was issued preventive orders from entering Chintapalli. It was as if his turn now to be under custody.

Nayudu's biography, Chatu Padya Mani Manjari, says that 500 Chenchus were killed on that night. The curses and cries of all those Chenchus and their families started playing with Nayudu's mind and also the entire Chintapalli estate. He reported the sightings of Chenchu souls everywhere in the Fort. This dastardly act made Nayudu unable to eat, sleep or have any peace. He was seeing maggots, human excrement in his food. The psychological troubles of Nayudu and many others were endless. It is written that God Shiva visited Nayudu in his dream, told him to leave Chintapalli immediately, and build Amaravati town as an act of penance[21].

Health has two sides to it – physical and mental health. Only when these two are in perfect balance would a human being be called fully healthy. Only then his humanity would bloom completely. When mental health is disturbed, then it will impact the whole well-being of humanity. History stands witness to this. Nayudu did everything in his capacity to regain his mental health. He performed innumerable Yajnas and Yagas. He made many offerings to Brahmins across his Samsthana. As part of one such act, he was told to get a big cow made entirely in gold, sit in its womb and come out of it. This act would render him, Cow Born. Hindu scriptures say that those who have seen the cow's womb are washed off of all sins. After this act, the sinless newborn should donate this golden cow to the Brahmins and lead a new life henceforth[22].

After doing everything as per the instructions, the time for donating the golden cow to the Brahmins came. A group of Madiga caste members rose and objected to the donation. As the golden cow is lifeless, and as all dead animals belong to Madigas as per societal norms, this golden cow also belongs to Madiga's and hence cannot be donated to Brahmins, they declared. If the King proceeds with the donation, all the dead animals in the Samsthana should be given to Brahmins, they warned. Unable to counter their claims, the King opened his Coffers and brought gold equal in weight to the cow, donated it to the Brahmins, in addition to giving away the cow to the Madiga's.

History – Tall Claims and Falsifications

Vijayaditya Narendra ruled Raj Mahendra Varam for 48 years. He went on 108 conquests and built 108 Shiva temples. The Kunti Madhavalaya Temple, situated in Pithapuram, was built by him. Prolaya Vemareddi got 108 Shiva Temples built at the same time across his kingdom [23]. Just like them, Venkatadri Nayudu too aimed to build 108 temples. But the "Kaifiyats" mention that he got only nine temples built finally. Eight temples were built on the eight sides of Chaturmukha Temple [24].

Philosophy says that "Knowing the Ultimate Truth" is the biggest accomplishment for a human being. When I read that Nayudu got 108 temples, 108 lakes, the Amaravathi Fort, and the Amaravathi town built, I felt that he is truly a great man. When I went into details, all I could find are the details of only nine temples built. Two Hundred years have passed after his period, and popular literature still mentions the lies and tall claims as truths about Nayudu. Who is cheating whom here?

Nayudu's biography claims that 108 temples were built. Some British records mention 180 temples. Kodali Books mentions that the number of Chenchus killed was 500. Mackenzie's records show the number 150 when the reality is that the temples built were mere 9, not 108, or 180. Aren't the history books, including the British resorting to manipulating history?

Nayudu amassed great wealth as if thinking that his life is permanent and this wealth would give him the ultimate happiness in his life. It was not so. All his wealth brought him more and more woes, sufferings, and sadness.

Amaravathi: A Pail of Diamond Dust

It is a fact that Venkatadri Nayudu renovated part of Amareshvara temple, whereas several history books credit Nayudu with the building of the temple entirely. Nayudu built a fort near the Amareshvara Temple, which lead to the formation of Amaravathi Town there. The Sthoopa that was there at the site of Amaravathi Fort was known as "Deepala Dinne – Mound of Lamps". When the Fort was being built, Deepala Dinne was broken up and used as bricks in the new construction [25].

The Amaravathi Sthoopa was a venerated Bauddha structure from the year 200 BC. It was an important Buddhist landmark in South India. Such an important Buddhist structure looked like mere limestone bricks to Hindu ruler Venkatadri Nayudu [26]. The construction of Amaravathi town led to uncontrolled excavation and pillage of the historical artefacts. Many precious sculptures and other articles were moved out of India and sold in British markets by Samuel Johnston's team.

In a society built on money, man would stoop to any levels to amass it. He would not hesitate to commit any harsh act; neither would he think of any morals. Human values like kindness, compassion, justice, sense of right and wrong would entirely disappear. Greed for wealth would kill all wisdom. Ego would rule over the senses. Even if they face any punishments, wisdom would be far from them. They would never think of correcting their mistakes; learning from others would also be ruled out. They would always be thinking of new crimes to gain more wealth.

Buddhist traveller Tavernier wrote that he saw a diamond in a mine in Kolluru village and described it as a 36 Mangalene (663/8 carat) weighing, clear, beautiful diamond [27]. The Kohinoor diamond is an invaluable treasure of Telugu Heritage. Tummala Seetarama Murthi, who wrote a song called "Salutations to you, Oh Mother Goddess of Telugu, salutes to you, Mother India..." described like this:

"The Kohinoor of Kollur is the flower in your hairdo...

The Kolar Mines are your treasure...."

The Kohinoor diamond was mined in Kolluru village, Sattenapalli Taluq, Gunturu district. It was shifted to Northern India by Malik Kapoor in the 13th Century. Strangely, it is now a family heirloom of the British Empire, given to the eldest daughter-in-law of the family by the matriarch. Indian Government has made several requests to the British Government to hand over its treasure back, but the British have been denying it, showing the flimsiest of reasons every time [28].

Search for Buried Gold

After Nayudu left Chintapalli fort, he was at Amaravathi for six months and another six months at Chebrolu. Nayudu's men found a treasure of silver and few golden coins when he was in Chebrolu. Mackenzie and Borrayya had concluded that the ancient Temple in Tadikonda had a big treasure under it. Mackenzie was already settled in Amaravathi by then, searching for diamond mines[29]. As per their instructions, Nayudu organized excavations at three sites near Tadikonda Temple epigraph.

Diggings were made on the South, North, and East sides of the Tadikonda Epigraph at considerable depth[30]. It was as if the Chintapalli King Nayudu had become a gold digger under the influence of some people and was looking for a measly bucket of gold.

Some Deeds are Difficult to Forget

The mental anguish that took over Nayudu's mind after the Chenchu massacre never let go of him. He could not forget his treachery and could never forgive himself for the grave crime he committed. Happiness was a distant memory; a peaceful night sleep was a luxury that could he not afford. He would remain alone in his room throughout the day, brooding over his misdeeds. He would think of penance that would bring him out of this misery. But his crimes were so big that he was unable to come out of the depths. Around that time, adding to his woes, his daughter died in a fatal fall from the Fort's outer wall. As he was afraid that he might die without any son to carry his name, he decided to adopt one of his close relatives. After due consideration, he adopted his cousin Chandramouli's son, Jagannadha Babu. But his wife Verremamba did not like that kid much. So he adopted another cousin, Naganna's son Raghunadha Babu also.

Despite his search for peace and comfort, Nayudu could not forget the wails of Chenchus and the blood that he shed on that cruel night. With his heart full of grief that would never leave him, Venkatadri Nayudu died at an inopportune age of 55.

The results of one's acts (also known as Karma) come to experience in two ways:

1) Within the lifetime, with every minute of existence reminding the acts one has committed;

2) In the next life, where the punishment might be equally severe, but without the knowledge of the reasons for the fate.

✸✸✸

These Are Facts You Are Reading

In the year 1794, the British reorganized their administration and established the system of Collectorates. Accordingly, the Godavari district was formed with three divisions. Kakinada was the centre for the first division, Mogalturu for the second, and Rajamandri for the third division. All these divisions were under the Machilipatnam Collectorate.

The famine during the years 1791-95 had a severe impact on the area of Machilipatnam Collectorate. With thousands of deaths and a lack of food grains, all the Samsthanas of the area had huge pending taxes to the British. Under pressure from Madras Presidency, Collector Oaks insisted the Samsthanas of his area to pay up their dues. The Madras Presidency appointed Mackenzie as the special officer to collect all the tax dues.

As per Mackenzie's orders, Vennelakanti Subbarao and Borrayya worked together to collect tax dues from Char Mahal and Selam Samsthanas[31]. Upon a new scheme proposed by Vennelakanti, Collector Munro and Mackenzie approved a plan to relocate families of the Pakanati clan who were expert farmers to Krishna, Godavari districts.

Nadu's – Regions

The folk songs gathered by Acharya Donappa mention that Paka Nadu/ Poka Nadu (Pogi Rashtra) is the region that begins between Penna River bed and Gundlakamma River and spread over Veli Gonda through Budvel, Rajam Pet Taluqs of Kadapa district. The Ancient Andhra History and Geography books describe the Nellore district area with Penna River as the front and stretching on to the south side is are Pakanadu. The Northern area of this place consists of Kandukur, Venkatagiri and Udayagiri Taluqs.

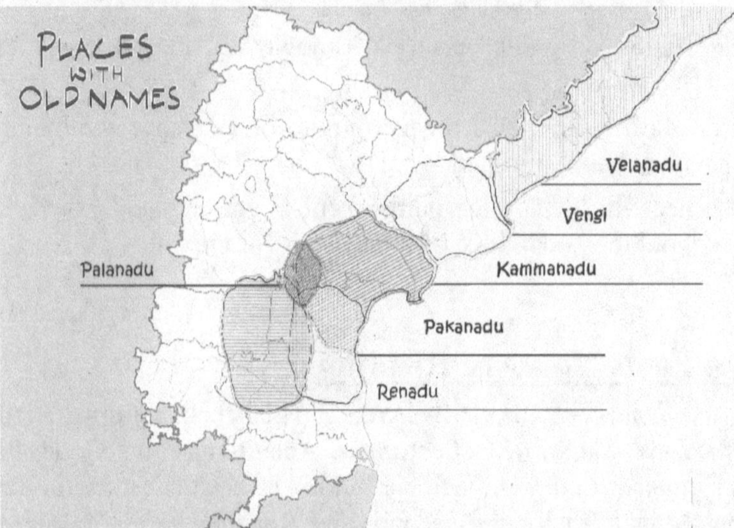

Pakanadu was also known as "Poongi Rashtra". Pakanadu was a part of Udayagiri rule during the Vijaya Nagara Empire period as per found epigraphs [32]. "Nadu" is a word used to suggest an area/ region.

Renadu	Kadapa, Kurnool and Nallamala forest region.
Palnadu (Pallavanadu)	The area from Macherla to Gurjala
Kammanadu (Karmarashtram)	The region between Guntur and Manneru rivers.
Vengi (Vegi)	The region between Godavari and Krishna rivers.
Velanadu	The region between Katakam (Cuttack) and Pithapuram.

Samsthanas and Etymology of Caste Names

According to the "Bethi Reddy Legend" from the Kakatiya period, the name "Kapu" in the Andhra region suggests a caste that protected the society by standing guard – Kapu. Earlier, there were four branches in this caste – "Kamma, Velama, Balija, and Reddy." At the time of the census, the British separated the Kapu caste into four sects.

The word "Chaudhari" has been in existence since 1580 AD. "Chaudhari" denotes a job title that took care of local business dealings. It slowly turned into a honorific before finally settling down as a caste name. "Nayudu" emerged from the word "Nayakudu". The Nayaka kings who ruled Thanjavur were referred to as "Nayudu's. As the word "Nayudu" was taken by Balija, Telaga, and Kapu castes. Kamma caste people took over "Chaudhari" for themselves. Devarakota and Muktyala Samsthanas were under Kamma rule.

Velamas are strong financially and socially. The occupation of their caste is wielding the stick and sword. Telugu lands have two kinds of Velamas – Padma Velamas and Adi Velamas. The womenfolk of Padma Velama's follow the veil (Parada or Ghosha) system. Bobbili, Nujiveedu, Char Mahal, Pithapuram Samsthanas were under the Velama rule. Samineni Muddu Narasimha Naidu was a Velama The book "HitaSoochani" (1855) that was written on him presents him as a scholar who worked on developing education in general and Telugu language in particular[33]. He was one of the earliest rationalists and a reformist also.

The Brahmins in Telugu lands mostly belonged to Vaidika, Niyogi, Smartha, Madhva, Vaishnava, Shaiva, Dravida, and Golkonda writers' branches. The Niyogi Brahmins took care of soldierly duties, worked as ministers for local rulers, worked as village-level bookkeepers administering land revenue collections and disbursals. Eluru's MantriPragada and Polavaram were Brahmana Samsthanas.

The Reddy caste was primarily agrarian. Pakanati, Renati, Motati, Velanati, Gudati, Panta (Desati), Pedakanti, Kuncheti, Oruganti, Bhumanchi were the most known branches of this caste in the region. Some of these names were formed based on their domicile and others based on the specific customs they followed. They used to carry Reddy, Rao, Bahaddur, etc., as honorifics with their names [34].

Palegars of the Adopted Mandals

The Palegar ruling system in the Adopted Mandals is known to have been in vogue since the Krishna Deva Raya period. The Palegars were originally deployed as intermediaries to collect taxes from the farmers. Once the Adopted Mandals – Pakanadu, Renadu, Kurnool, Bellari – went into British ownership, the equation between the British Crown and the Palegars turned sour. It was simmering like a volcano that was ready to burst any moment. Around that time, Thomas Munro was appointed as the Collector to mainly focus on streamlining British India's Taxation System and collecting the enhanced taxes without fail from the public. He eyed the riches amassed by the Palegars and declared the removal of the Palegar System entirely, and offered a monthly honorarium to outgoing Palegars to placate them.

Munro schemed against the Palegars for eight years and pushed them to severe extremities during that period. Those Palegars who opposed him – about 80 of them were captured and held in Guttikota for many years. British Army, under the leadership of Major General Campbell, occupied all the important Palegar forts.

The Kapu's and Niyogi Brahmins of the Adopted Mandals looked after the agriculture and Land Management duties. Munro looked into these sections of Kapus and Niyogis particularly. As an expert in psychological warfare, Munro concocted a scheme to reduce public support for the Palegars and offered arable lands to the public from other areas to settle in these regions. As part of this plan, the Niyogi Brahmins, Reddy's, Kamma's, Golla's, Mala's of Pakanadu region were accommodated in the Nujiveedu, Char Mahal, Challapalli, Pithapuram Samsthanas of Sarkar districts. Similarly, some were sent to the Vanaparthi, Gadwal, Kamareddi Samsthanas of the Hyderabad state.

Four Sub Collectors were given this task exclusively. These Sub Collectors used their powers in Adhavani (Adoni), Halpanakalli, Kurnool, Pakanadu, Renadu regions for this large relocation. Thus Munro used all the tricks in his books to neck out the Palegars from the system. Some of those Palegars took refuge in forests, regrouped and tried their best to fight the British army. Most of them realized that their efforts may not yield much and got into some of the other settlements of grants, honorariums with the British and withdrew their revolt.

<u>Paka Nadu – A Region of Thirteen Villages</u>

The Pakanadu society that was shifted to the Northside prepared themselves to assimilate in the new area and lead a proper life. But the memory of their ancestral land still lived in their hearts and created anguish in them. The alien status in the new lands troubled them from time to time and left scars in their psyche.

List of the villages where the British abandoned the Pakanati Reddy's.

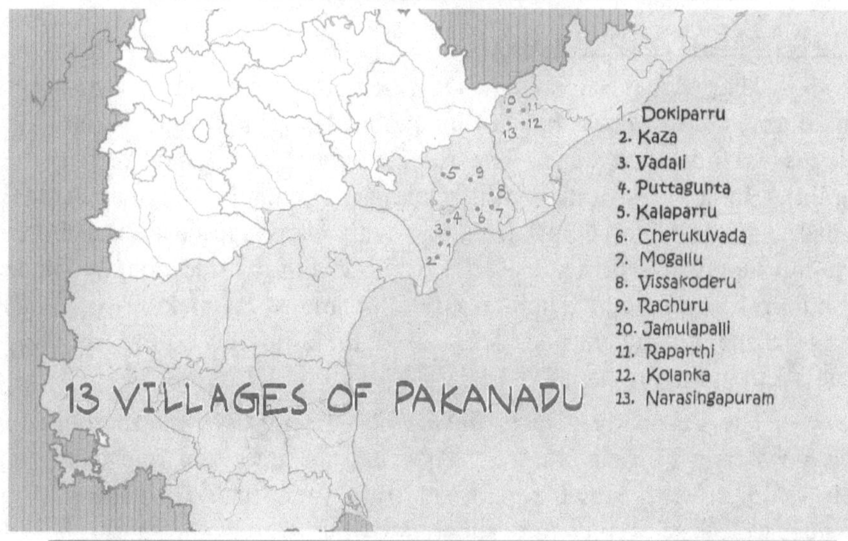

Village	Sansthan	District
Dokiparru	Char-Mahal Sansthan (Guraja)	Krishna District
Kaaja	Devarakota Sansthan (Challapalli)	Krishna District
Vadali	Char-Mahal Sansthan (Guraja)	Krishna District
Puttagunta	Char-Mahal Sansthan (Guraja)	Krishna District
Kalaparru	Mantri Pregada Sansthan (Eluru)	Krishna District
Cherakuvada	Char-Mahal Sansthan (Guraja)	Krishna District
Mogollu	Char-Mahal Sansthan (Guraja)	Krishna District
Vissakoderu	Char-Mahal Sansthan (Guraja)	Krishna District
Rachuru	Mantri Pregada Sansthan (Eluru)	Krishna District
Jamulapalli	Pithapuram Sansthan	Godavari District
Raparthi	Pithapuram Sansthan	Godavari District
Kolanka	Pithapuram Sansthan	Godavari District
Narasingapuram	Pithapuram Sansthan	Godavari District

Char Mahal Samsthana

Char Mahal Samsthana is the area comprising Krishna district's Kaikaluru, Gudivada Taluq's Vinnakota, Kalidindi, and Bittarajalli villages as four Paragana's. The ruler of the Samsthana lived in the Guraja village of Mudinepalli. Dokiparru village of Char Mahal Samsthana is a major agrarian village with many sub-castes related to farming supporting it. The "Peerla Sayibu" family traditionally made agricultural equipment. There used to be many "Dudekula" families living in the village earlier. They used to build the cotton spinning wheels and maintain them.

The Pakanadu society did its best to preserve the memory of their birth land in their children. They had an unwritten rule to marry their children with suitable partners from their native villages only. Because of the strict rules they adhered to, they were sometimes referred to as "Madi Redlu – Chaste Reddy's".

Sri Ganga Parvathi sametha Agasteshvara Sivalayam(1813), Dokiparru

The Agasteshvara Temple was the first Temple these Pakanati Reddy's built for them in the area. It was as if they prayed Lord Shiva to prevent any bad thing that might come their way and started owning up the place.

During festivals, they would gather at the Agasteshvara Temple with all their families. They would bring new crops of maize corn, green gram, and Rice; add some tamarind and cook it. They would prepare pickle using the coconuts offered to the deity, adding salt, tamarind and freshly grown chillies and crush under the big grinding stone in the temple to be had with the Khichdi.

All the kids of the village would go swimming in the two lakes of the village every day and eat fresh vegetable produce like corn cobs, green gram, cucumbers, etc., from the nearby fields. It is said that these two lakes were dug by a female family member of Nawab Basalat Jung, who took refuge in this village for some time when her life was under threat. As these two lakes were not enough for all the village needs, the Pakanati Reddy's suffered to meet all their farming needs in the initial years. After few years, they thought of digging more lakes to support their farming.

Digging Lakes

Pamireddy Linga Reddy learnt all the intricacies of farming from his father. He learnt basic education, enough to be able to write on paper. He learnt the "Amara Kosham" well enough to quote Vargu's, poems and shlokas freely. The names of Telugu years, months, weeks, tithi, nakshatra, festivals, auspicious times, etc., were well known to him. He learnt his value system from his genial father. His knowledge of all things connected to nature was commendable. He would talk only when necessary. He would help his wife Mallamma whenever needed.

When two male calves were born in their yard, he named them "Lava – Kusha." The calves grew up to be strong bulls that would carry any amount of weight in the cart. Linga Reddy trained them with carrying heavyweights like sand, stones, etc., to increase their stamina. They would respond to his voice and stand ready to run as per his command.

To accomplish any task, commitment to the task, a sense of duty, and the ability to assess the pros and cons of the methods chosen are necessary. The Pakanati families had these qualities in abundance. W ater is an essential source for agriculture. With this basic thought in mind, the Pakanati farmers made it a practice over the ages to observe the flow of rainwater on the terrain. They had also learnt to understand the nature of the soil and the right kind of crops for that soil. They had a clear division of physical and knowledge-based work. When they realized the need for more water resources in their new settlement, they decided upon digging new lakes. They identified the right locations for these lakes to benefit all farmers. Once they have finished the planning, they began digging these lakes with all community participating in it. The families would dig the lakes in summer and continue with routine farming in other seasons.

The first lake was Bhadra Reddy lake. The gravel that was removed in the digging was brought on bullock carts during the night to the Shivalayam and dumped there. The men would avoid tiring themselves and the animals in the hot sun and work only in the evenings and cool nights. Linga Reddy would work with Bulls Lava and Kusha in this menial activity. Once the cart bucket is filled with gravel, Linga Reddy would say, "It is enough now," the attentive bulls would listen to it and start moving to the temple to dump the soil. Once the soil is dumped after waiting in the queue, the bulls would go to the lake again to pick up the next round of gravel.

This activity would continue throughout the night. As the bulls were so well trained, they would do most of the job without any special monitoring. As the bulls were adorned with bells and cymbals in their necks, their steady, rocking movement would create music that would lull the master to sleep in the bucket.

Because life in those times was so in unison with nature, the animals, particularly cows and bulls that would help in farming, were treated as part of the family. People would continue to have more animals in their herd; selling them was not heard of. When a cow or bull passed away, it would be sent off in a grand ritual. They would bathe it properly; adorn it with turmeric and vermilion on the horns, nostrils, back and tail. Eyesalve was also applied. Kohl was applied on few other body parts to ward off the evil eye. The whole village would offer respect and send it off.

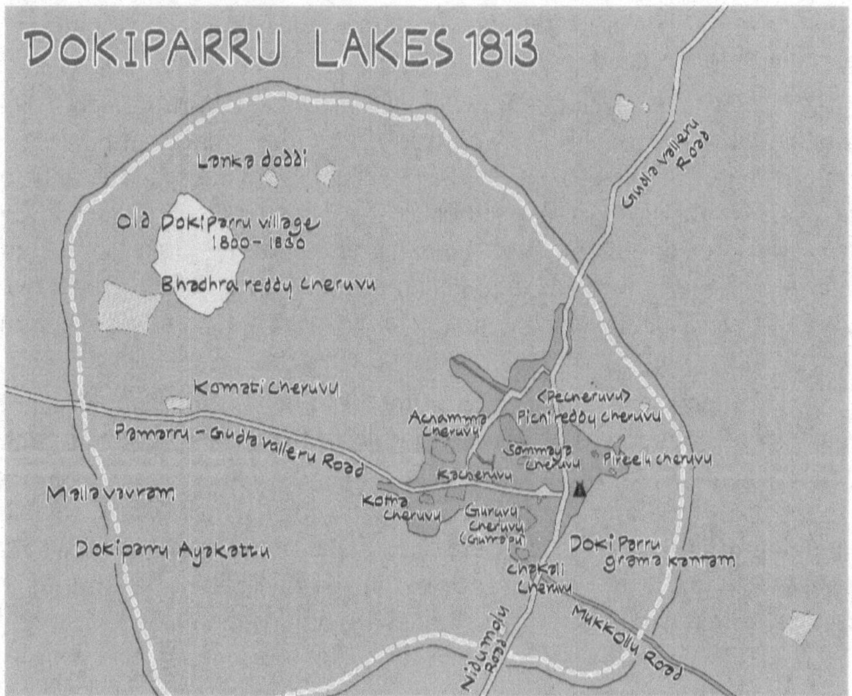

Together, all the villagers took up two summers and forty acres of area to build the Bhadra Reddy Tank. Next year, work on Komati Cheruvu was planned. Thus, in about a decade, eleven tanks were built – Bhadra Reddy, Komati, Guruvu (Gurrapu), Sommayya, Pitchi Reddy (Peccharapu), Pallalamma, Chakali, Acchamma, Piri, Mirjar, Kashemma (Kaccheruvu) lakes were built. Thus their dependence on rain and rain-related farming ended. They would judiciously use the water from these 11 tanks and grow crops year long. As they also focused on amassing herds of cows and bulls, they could increase their farming exponentially.

As per family legends, Pamireddy Linga Reddy, Kanumuri Ganapathi Reddy, participated in digging these tanks directly. The area of the total irrigation in the village was about four thousand acres. Once all the tanks were filled, they would hold enough water to sustain two years of farming and domestic needs.

What is a T.M.C?

A T.M.C is a thousand million cubic feet of water. That is, imagine one feet length, width, and height of an ice cube - it would equal one cubic foot of water. Hundred crores or thousand million such ice cubes put together would equal one T.M.C. A standard lake/ tank size would hold about one-tenth of T.M.C water. That means ten lakes would hold one T.M.C. of water, which would irrigate eight thousand acres of paddy farming. For crops that require less water, about twelve thousand acres could be irrigated.

As per this calculation, the eleven lakes Dokiparru villagers dug upheld more than one T.M.C of water. But the village still faced a drinking water problem. As the village was close to the sea, attempts to dig wells would mostly draw saltwater. The villagers were forced to go many miles for drinking water. Women could carry only one pot full of water at one time, whereas men would use a wooden yoke to carry two pots at a time. Due to social stigma, widows were forced to get water in the dark of the night when nobody would see them.

Villagers would grow sorghum, millets, and pumpkins for regular consumption. After making a hole in the pumpkin, green gram and jaggery would be filled in it and the entire pumpkin cooked in water for about a half-hour. That would be a regular breakfast. People belonging to "Erukala Caste" were the village future tellers who would predict the rainfall in the coming season during "Sodi – soothsaying" sessions, which would help in planning cropping patterns.

References

1. Sri Dasu Kesava Rao's "The Nallamalas-Emerald Paradise", Page:43
2. Dr. Mudiganti Sujathareddy, Book of "Charitraka Samajika Nepadyamlo Telugu Sahitya Charitra" Page:305
3. (i) G.Mackenzie, Kistna District Manual – P 338 ." Cavali Venkata Borayya, Son of Cavali Venkata Subbayya, was the well-known assistant of Colin Mackenzie, the Archaeologist.
    (ii) "Biographical Sketches Of Dekkan Poets" – Page: 154.
4. Dasu Vishnu Rao wrote in his genealogy that this information was in the footnote of a book written by Cambel. Dasu Vishnurao B.A.B.L was the son of great poet Dasu Sriramulu, Born in Dokiparru village (1876) in Krishna district.
5. Account of the Jains, collected from a priest of this sect at Mudgeri; Translated by Cavelly Boria, Brahmin: for Major C.Mackenzie-1809 Asiatic Researches vol 9.
6. G.Mackenzie, Kistna District Manual, P:309,310
7. Kodali Sri Lakshmi Narayana, "Book of Sri Raja Vankatadri Naidu" Page: 75
8. (i) Kodali Sri Lakshmi Narayana, "Book of Sri Raja Vankatadri Naidu" Page: 227
    (ii) G.Mackenzie, Kistna District Manual – P:311 – "The first step of this nephew,   Venkatadri son of Jaganna well known of Venkatadri Naidu, was to imprison in the Fort at Chintapalle his uncle's son Naganna alias Papayya and Chandramouli.

    Acharya *Kolakaluri Enoch* , Adi Andhrudu, page: 31,32
9. Acharya *Kolakaluri Enoch* , Adi Andhrudu, page: 18,19
10. (i) Kodali Sri Lakshmi Narayana, "Book of Sri Raja Vankatadri Naidu" Page: 112

    (ii) Guide to Guntur – P – 162 – 25-9-1791 – His offer to seize the robbers be accepted – Permission to Seize Chinnu Papayya Nayaka on 20-10-1791 – Maj. Burr and Zamindar's peons drove out the robbers on 11-11-1791
11. Ibid P - 202 "His village Kammalacheruvu was given to Vasireddy Venkatadri Naidu (Chenchu Village - Ploigar named Ramanayak)"
12. (i) G.Mackenzie – Kistna District Manual "From the Nizam, he obtained the title of Manuru Sultan, nominally because he extirpated robbers, but really in consideration of a lakh of Pagodas, sent."
    (ii) G. Mackenzie – Kistna District Manual – P – 171. "The most southerly village in these valleys Manne Sultan Palem, a name which commemorates the title bestowed by the Nizam upon the Chintapalli Zamindar for his prowess in subduing certain rebel poligars.

(iii) Kodali Sri Lakshmi Narayana, "Book of Sri Raja Vankatadri Naidu" Page: 115,116

13. Kodali Sri Lakshmi Narayana, "Book of Sri Raja Vankatadri Naidu" Page: 230

14. Kodali Sri Lakshmi Narayana, "Book of Sri Raja Vankatadri Naidu" Page: 92

15. Kodali Sri Lakshmi Narayana, "Book of Sri Raja Vankatadri Naidu" Page:211

16. Acharya *Kolakaluri Enoch,* Adi Andhrudu, page:11— "Commander Bhujanga Rao was asked to go to the forests and bring Chenchus as answers. The commander went and talked slowly with Ramadasu, the elder of Chanchus, and told him that Lord Venkatadri would take care without any problem, and they believed him. They were 500 people.

17. Kodali Sri Lakshmi Narayana, "Book of Sri Raja Vankatadri Naidu" Page:109

18. Veturi Prabhakarashastri, Chatupadya Manimanjari. Page 66, 67.

19. Kodali Sri Lakshmi Narayana, "Book of Sri Raja Vankatadri Naidu" Page:109

20. (i) Kodali Sri Lakshmi Narayana, "Book of Sri Raja Vankatadri Naidu" Page: 110,111

(ii) G. Mackenzie – Kistna District Manual. – P – 312. "It is said that during his energetic days, he had determined to get rid of Kistna District Manual, a tribe of Chenchus who pillaged his Zamindari and so, inviting 150 of the men of the tribe to a feast, he had them all beheaded. Remorse overwhelmed him for his treachery, and whenever he sat down to his meals, the grain turned into insects – such as the popular legend."

21. (i) Kodali Sri Lakshmi Narayana, "Book of Sri Raja Vankatadri Naidu" Page:166.

(ii) Acharya *Kolakaluri Enoch* , Adi Andhrudu, page: 21,22.

22. (i) G. Mackenzie – Kistna District Manual – P.11 – "Polaya VemaReddi dedicated 108 temples to the worship of Siva".

(ii) Kodali Sri Lakshmi Narayana, "Book of Sri Raja Vankatadri Naidu" Page:125.

23. Kodali Sri Lakshmi Narayana, "Book of Sri Raja Vankatadri Naidu" Page:175.

24. Kodali Sri Lakshmi Narayana, "Book of Sri Raja Vankatadri Naidu" Page:120.

25. (i) Kodali Sri Lakshmi Narayana, "Book of Sri Raja Vankatadri Naidu" Page:121.

(ii) Ibid – P -164. "It was Rajah Vasireddy Venkatadri Naidu who, in searching for building materials, first laid open the famous Buddhist cravings at Amaravathi, so well-known now to savants all over the world." "It was in digging to obtain stone for these buildings that the

Rajah's people unearthed a portion of the famous Buddhist ruins at Amaravathi, first described by Colin Mackenzie.

26. (i) Kodali Sri Lakshmi Narayana, "Book of Sri Raja Vankatadri Naidu" Page:121.

(ii) Ibid – P -164. "It was Rajah Vasireddy Venkatadri Naidu who, in searching for building materials, first laid open the famous Buddhist cravings at Amaravathi, so well-known now to savants all over the world." "It was in digging to obtain stone for these buildings that the Rajah's people unearthed a portion of the famous Buddhist ruins at Amaravathi, first described by Colin Mackenzie."

27. Kodali Sri Lakshmi Narayana, "Book of Sri Raja Vankatadri Naidu" Page:136.

28. (i) Bharati Monthly Magazine – 1938 – Volume 10.

(ii) Sri Digavalli Sivarao, "Kathalu-Gathalu" Part2,Kohinoor Vajram.

29. Kodali Sri Lakshmi Narayana, "Book of Sri Raja Vankatadri Naidu" Page:126.

30. (i) G.Mackenzie – Kistna District Manual - P.204 – "Some workmen came upon a treasure consisting of several masses of molten gold as bricks."

(ii) Kodali Sri Lakshmi Narayana, "Book of Sri Raja Vankatadri Naidu" Page:174.

31. (i) Ri. Krishna District manual, Page: 339.

(ii) Akkiraju Ramapati Rao, "The life of Vennelakanti Subbarao" 1873, page: 47. "On 1st June 1823, we left Achanta and sailed through the inns at Shringavriksham, Elurupadu, Dokiparru, and Muvavva. On 3rd June 1823, we crossed the Krishna River and reached Kolluru. Here, we went to a house whose surname is Balijepalli."

32. (i) A Manual of the Kurnool District Narahari GopalaKristnamah Chetty Madras 1886, Page: 138

(ii) "Ancient Historical Geography" pages. 207-211

33. G. Parameswaran Pillai "Representation Men of South India," Pages: 148-149

34. (i) Jogendranath Bhattacharya, Hindu Castes and Tribes",1896.

(ii) Brian E. Hemphill, Bioanthropology of the Hindu Kush Borderlands, A Dental Morphology Investigation, Page:203

PAKANATI MOONLIGHT DAZZLE

How Ambrosia Turns into Poison

After Vasireddi Venkatadri Nayudu's death in the year 1816, Chintapalli Samsthana was split in between Jagannadha Babu (314 villages) and Ramanadha Babu (237) villages. Jagannadha Babu also got 50 lakh rupees, 5 lakh Savarans of gold, and one lakh pounds sterling as part of the inheritance [35]. As the saying goes that anything in excess turns into poison, Jagannadha Babu and Ramanadha Babu often quarrelled about the differences in their inheritance. The complaints would be that Jagannadha Babu got more villages, and Ramanadha Babu got more income from his villages, and the quarrel would never stop. Both claimed more rights over the erstwhile undivided Samsthana and demand more income and power. Gradually they approached civil courts for all and sundry things, paid lakhs on these legal disputes, and within two years declared that both have gone bankrupt. But the legal disputes continued for another thirty years, yielding no definitive outcome [36].

The Web of Lies beneath the Power

Pindaris were highway robbers who came in hordes from Marathi lands and wreaked havoc along their path. The word Pindari came from "Pindra", which meant an intoxicating drink in Marathi. These Pindari teams would rob people, kidnap kids, intoxicate them with a drink, carry them back, hiding them in haystacks and sell them as slaves. The number of these dreaded Pindaris grew from 10 thousand to 30 thousand within 1815-16. Nellore and Krishna districts of Andhra Pradesh were the major targets of their attacks [37]. The local Samsthana rulers and also the British Army had sleepless nights because of them

How can the Nallamala Chenchus become Pindari's? While Venkatadri Nayudu dubbed Chenchus as thieves, the British started calling them Pindari's from 1816. It was probably an attempt at justifying their old atrocities against the poor tribals. But the time difference between the Chenchu massacre and the Pindari menace in these areas was at least two decades.

The Chenchu Grudge – Attempts for Revenge

Venkanna was a native of Akumalla village near Koyilakuntla. At an early age, He lost his parents. As an orphan, he was always restless and would wander all around, finally settling with the Chenchus of the Nallamala forest. A devout Hindu, he was a Shaivite who dressed as an ascetic all his life. He considered himself a Chenchu, followed their lifestyle, learned naturopathy from them, hypnosis tricks, and some of the Chenchus practice. Slowly he transformed into a religious guru and became Gosayi Venkanna. He played an instrumental role in turning the Chenchu enmity with Venkatadri Nayudu into a patriotic fight against British rule. He had also taught patience to the Chenchus to wait for the opportune time to strike Nayudu and the British.

Munro's Fear of Death

Thomas Munro was born on 27th May 1761 in Scotland. He joined the Madras regiment as a foot soldier in the year 1789. After Tippu Sultan's death, he was appointed the Collector of Adopted Mandals. In that position, he brought many Palegars onto their knees and increased the Company's income two folds. He resigned from his job briefly, went to England, and returned as Governor of Madras Residency on 08th Jun 1820.

The Chenchus would try to scare off any British officers travelling through their areas with supernatural tricks. British officers travelling to Gutti through Kurnool, Kadapa forests became victims of these attempts often. A Captain Newbolt, going this way, reported seeing a skull hanging from a tree near Pacharla [38]. Another British officer reported ash smeared tamarind falling into his carriage.

Governor Munro was once going to Gutti through these forests. Through his palanquin, he saw a shining, golden festoon on a tree. When he asked the Boya Palanquin carriers about it, an old Boya said that such garlands appear only to persons whose death is approaching them. Munro, who had seen many jwars and caused many deaths, got shaken up to his core, and the fear of death engulfed his thoughts. Though a devout Christian, this fear of death made him donate a big silver tumbler as an offering to Tirumala Venkateswara Swami. His donation is still part of the TTD's list of valuables.

Munro had earlier released a Gazette declaring that Hindu Mutts without any successors would belong to the British Crown after the due course. To oversee the implementation of this order, he went to visit Ahobilam Raghavendra Swami Mutt. It is not known what happened there, but he withdrew his Gazette immediately after the visit. Within six months, on 06th Jun 1827, Munro died of cholera near Pattikonda.

Uyyalavada Narasimha Reddy

The region between Kadapa's Jammala Madugu and Kurnool's Kovela Kuntla was ruled by Nossam Palegars (Chenchu Reddys). Uyyalavada Narasimha Reddy belonged to the Nossam area's Motati Reddy community[39]. The Kurnool district manual says that Nossam Palegar Chenchu Jayarami Reddy fought strongly outside the Markapuram Tahasildar office, opposing the handing over of Adopted Mandals to the British by Tippu Sultan in the year 1800. As per the twisted British policy, those who opposed the British would be termed as tax defaulters, thieves, and measures would be announced to punish them. The same tactic was applied on Nossam Command too. Their allegations and false propaganda continued for some time, making Nossam rulers face dire circumstances, dishonour.

This abasement, derogation led Majjari Narasimha Reddy to revolt against the British. The Uyyalavada Endowment generally yielded up to 30 thousand rupees income. The British unilaterally declared the impounding of the endowment and announced a pension (Tavarji) of 70 rupees only to the entire family. Narasimha Reddy's share in that would be about "11 rupees and 10 annas, 8 paise" only! In June 1846, When Narasimha Reddy sent his employee to collect his pension, the Tahasildar was said to have commented, "A servant, to another servant…" and sent off the employee without paying the pension. Reddy could not digest this insult and decided to take revenge [40].

Gosayi's Blessings

Gosayi Venkanna observed the discord Reddy felt on the British and encouraged his spirit of freedom whenever he can. When Reddy came to take part in the "Renadu Festival", Gosayi made Reddy repeat his promise that he would not go back on his word (for revolt). They may not have realized that this would lead to India's first struggle for independence against the British. Around that time, the British took custody of 23 estates that had no successors. In reality, only two estates among them were such – Nossam and Gundladurthi. As Reddy was planning to oppose the British, all the Kattubadidars – Palegars dispossessed of their Inams joined him in the revolt. Vanaparthi Raja Rameshwar Rao, Munagala Ramakrishna Reddy, Jataprolu Raja Lakshmana Rayudu, Penugonda, Avuku Jamindars, Hyderabad's Salam Khan, Kurnool's Papa Khan, Banagane Palle Nawab Mohammad Ali Khan joined forces with Narasimha Reddy. Of the nine thousand or so army that assembled, most were Nallamala Chenchus. That is why this army was also known as "Ellapula Ranuva".

Narasimha Reddy's army constructed several defending fortresses as part of their campaign, used cannons too. The area of this warfare was spread through Kottakota near Giddaluru to Uyyalavada and Koyilakuntla area – mostly within the Nallamala region. Visitors can still see one cannon used by Reddy's army that the British did not carry with them of the total 19 [41]. In his report to the British authorities, Collector Cochrane mentioned that Gosayi Venkanna blessed Narasimha Reddy that victory was assured to him in this fight. It is his instigation that led Reddy to revolt, wrote Cochrane.

The British sent their units under the leadership of Captain Knot and Captain Watson. Special Officer Norton gave additional tactical support from the Giddaluru centre. The Chenchu army chief was Obanna. In one faceoff at Giddaluru, hundreds of soldiers died on both sides. Chenchu Obanna cut Captain Norton's head and gifted it to Gosayi Venkanna.

The British declared Narasimha Reddy the enemy of the Crown and announced an award of Thousand rupees for capturing him. It was increased to two thousand soon, Ten thousand next. Cash awards were declared to capture team members Gosayi Venkanna, Obanna, Karnam Ashvathama, Dasari Roshi Reddy, Jangam Mallayya, and others.

The cash prize lured Narasimha Reddy's brother Malla Reddy to turn traitor and leak his whereabouts to the British. Narasimha Reddy's family aide Janakamma fed him food laced with intoxicants, leading to the capture of Narasimha Reddy. Reddy and his family were shifted to Kadapa under heavy military protection. Over 900 were charged with various crimes and tried. 112 persons were given jail terms. Some were banished to faraway islands.

On 09th Jan 1847, Narasimha Reddy had declared a traitor and was sentenced to be hanged till death. The judgment was carried out at Jurreti on 22nd Feb 1847. Thousands thronged to see it that day. Collector Cochrane administered Reddy's hanging himself. His severed head was hung up on the fort wall for over thirty years as a deterrent to others who might think of revolting [42].

Questions that Still Remain unanswered

What were the root causes of this revolt against the British? Over 5 thousand Chenchu, Boya, Yanadi sect warriors risked their lives in this fight. Why? Is it just because of Narasimha Reddy's leadership? How many Chenchus were exiled from the mainland after this fight? Historians should find answers to many such questions surrounding this important event. More facts will be in the limelight.

***

The Nandana Famine

The famine that struck in the year "Nandana" claimed two lakh lives in the Krishna district alone. From the six-lakh population of Kakinada and Rajahmundry districts, three lakhs died, while two lakhs from the five-lakh population of the Guntur district perished. The starvation that followed led to severe malnutrition, and people were forced to eat whatever that came their way, including roots and tubers that were probably poisonous, which led to more demises. The undernourishment weakened people so much that the stomachs were touching their backs; hence, the name "Dokkala Karuvu" was attached about that season.

Madras High Court Dubasi/ translator Enugula Veeraswami wrote about this drought in detail in his book "Kashi Yatra Charitra".

Rajahmundry Collector C.P.Brown also wrote about this period and brought it to the notice of the wider world. The British India government felt ashamed due to this negative publicity and forced Brown to resign from his job. Brown left for London in the year 1834 after his resignation.To prevent conditions like this from happening again, the British planned a barrage to Godavari River at Rajahmundry's Dhavaleshvaram. Sir Arthur Cotton was posted to oversee the construction of this barrage.

Sacred Godavari

A river is the flow of life itself. The evolution of humanity has been intertwined with the flow of rivers from time immemorial. Rivers change their course of flow from time to time. Human genius has been finding ways to counter such problems from time to time. The Hindu way of life says that life is composed of five basic elements – air, water, fire, earth and ether. Rig Veda also says that life was born in water.

River Godavari is one of the oldest rivers in the country. It is mentioned along with the most sacred rivers Ganga, Yamuna, and Saraswati in all the important scriptures. Born in the Western Ghats, at Trayambakam of Nasik district in Maharashtra, Godavari flows east side for 1350 kilometres before merging in the Bay of Bengal. All the tributaries of Godavari join with the main branch within the 1200 kilometres distance and form the mammoth Godavari, which breaks into two sections near Dhavaleshvaram. The eastern branch is called Gautami, and the western is Vashishtha.

Farming experts have come up with the system of inundation farming long ago to reduce dependence on rain. Rivers and streams that flow from hills would come to spate from time to time. Just before they overflow, trees would be cut, rocky boulders would be pushed against the flow, forming a barrier that would cause excess water to flow in waves from above this barrage. This thin wave of water flow is called "Vaaka"; because it would be formed against canals and rivers, it is called "Eruvaaka". In scientific terms, this is 'inundation farming'.

Mahishmathi – Kartaveeryarjunudu

Kaartaveeryarjuna, son of Krutaveerya, was the ruler of Mahishmathi Puram. A King of the Haihaya Clan, Kartaveerya was a ferocious warrior with thousand arms. Once, he stopped the river's flow with his thousand arms, forming a deeper tank of water for his wives to enjoy swimming. Rakshasa King Ravana, who was bathing downstream, was surprised by the sudden stop in water flow. When he was told the reason, he became angry at the mischief played by Kartaveerya and challenged him to fight. Kartaveerya looked at the ten-headed Ravana like an insect and tossed him like a toy among his wives to play with. Later, he took Ravana to his capital Mahishmathi as a prisoner and earned the title "Ravana Vijetha".

Arthur Thomas Cotton

Parashurama subjugated this very same Kartaveerya when he took Sage Jamadagni's sacred cow by force. Kartaveerya could not take this defeat in the hands of a Brahmin ascetic; he abandoned his kingdom, roamed around as a wanderer, and let go of his life force in the Western Ghats near the place river Godavari was born later. The Hindu scriptures mention this tale to teach that stopping the flow of rivers in any method is harmful. This belief took deep roots, and Hindu progeny has mostly refrained from building barrages across any flow of water [43]. Interestingly, the same society has grown to believe that the "Pushkara season" – or the time of spate that comes for rivers every 12 years, is very sacred and rushes to bathe in the respective rivers during that time in great multitudes.

Thomas Arthur Cotton

Arthur Cotton was a workaholic who looked at his work as the highest form of worship. His dedication and commitment were the only reasons to fulfil the dream of the Dhavaleshvaram on Godavari [44]. And it created the green carpet that formed the 'rice bowl of India', "Kona Seema – Coastal Belt" here. This barrage has led to the complete changeover in the lives and livelihood of people living in this vast area. The population here in 1846 was 5 lakhs 60 thousand; by 1891, it grew to 20 lakhs 70 thousand. It was as if the land itself was spawning these multitudes. In 1844, all the revenues together from this area amounted to 17 lakhs 25 thousand and 841 rupees only. Only the land revenue in 1898 was fourfold - 60 lakhs 19 thousand and 224 rupees as per records!

Along with working on the Godavari Delta system, Cotton's team had also managed to get all the planning and permissions for a barrage on the Krishna River at Vijayawada by 1851. It was named "Krishna Delta Work." By 1855, the Krishna Barrage was also completed, which rendered the whole region between Krishna and Godavari forever green. Next ten years, Cotton's team spent on digging all the canals and tributaries and other management systems that would take water to all regions. In the year 1858, Cotton had proposed linking all the major 24 rivers in the country.

The Creaking Cot

This is an anecdote from the time when Cotton attended the interview in the Engineering department. Along with Cotton, two more candidates were selected for the next in-depth interviews and were told to stay there overnight. They were given separate rooms and comfortable cots etc. Two candidates slept peacefully as soon as they had their dinner. But Cotton could not sleep immediately as the cot was creaking a lot with every twist and turn. Cotton felt that something was wrong with the cot and got down to inspect it. He noticed a Pound coin under one of the cot legs, which created an imbalance and caused the creaking noise. Cotton removed it and then could sleep peacefully as the noise disappeared.

The next morning, when interviews began again, they were all asked whether they could sleep well. Two candidates said that everything was good, and they slept very well. Arthur Cotton pulled out the Pound Coin from his pocket and explained his observations. Cotton was selected for the job. It was his curiosity, observation of imbalance that landed Cotton the job as an engineer who went on to build barrages on both Godavari and Krishna Rivers.

Truth is always Great

The population of Dokiparru increased in proportion with the improved farming conditions in the area. The area where all the gravel from the newly dug tanks was dumped became a landmass slightly higher than the rest of the village. The villagers considered it better for building their homes and made it their main dwelling area. The plateau between the east and northeast side of Acchamma lake, Pallalamma lake, up to Pirila lake, was turned into a residential zone. The increased availability of water made them shift to paddy growing. Different snacks and condiments made of rice like ulavacharu, puffed rice balls, arisalu, badusha, jangri, jilebi, idli, and other strength-giving food varieties became common households. Houses in those times were mud houses made from the rich alluvial soil common in the region. Such houses stay cool in hot summer weather also. Big windows and benches in front of houses were a common feature.

Because of the regular supply of water from the tanks, there was no predicament of a crop failure. Hence the payment of taxes would happen regularly in the area. The village elders like Pamireddy Linga Reddy would handle tax collection and submission to the Char

Mahal Samsthana authorities promptly. Even during the dreaded Nandana Famine, tax collection from the area did not fail. Few farmers suggested that they should defer tax submission during the famine as most villages were also not paying up their taxes. But Linga Reddy refused the suggestion, saying that being truthful holds great value, particularly to a farmer who is so connected to Mother Nature. He was ready to face the disgruntled complaints of few farmers for this honesty.

Linga Reddy had a son very late in his life named Nagireddy.

Kashi Yatra – Pakanati Traveler House in History

Two Pakanati Niyogi Brahmins – Vennelakanti Subbarao and Enugula Veeraswami mentioned the Dokiparru Traveler's Rest House in their Kashi travelogues. They both mentioned that during their return journey from Kashi, they rested at the Dokiparru Rest House for few days and proceeded to Madras via Kolluru of Krishna district.

Veeraswami's Kashi Travelogue describes the events of 15 months, 15 days, and 15 hours. Vennelakanti Subba Rao was related to Enugula Veeraswami and Kavali Brothers too. He stayed at Kavali Venkata Lakshmayya in Calcutta in the year 1823 during his journey of Kashi. Colin Mackenzie was working in Calcutta during those days. The Kashi Yatra travelogues written by Veeraswami and Subbarao describe the events of their trip to Kashi that happened in different years, but most of the details of the journey match. Their stay at Dokiparru Travel Lodge was also one of the coherent events.

Learning Telugu is a Must

Madras Governor Thomas Munro passed an order that each British Officer must learn at least one Indian local language. C.P.Brown started learning Telugu from the time he started working as an Assistant Collector at Kadapa district. He had worked as Collector at Machilipatnam for three years and also at Rajahmundry. He gained a good knowledge of the Krishna, Godavari Delta during this period (1829-34). As his command over Telugu increased, he

C.P Brown

attempted to translate many Telugu classics into English. Vemana's history, Vemana's Poems, a compilation of a many-volume Telugu/ English dictionary, and iconic Telugu books. His work for Telugu is hailed as a great service by any Englishman even now.

References

35. (i) G.Mackenzie – Krishna District Manual – P.314 – "Jagannatha Babu, on his father's death, got possession of a hoard of 50 lakhs of rupees and a million sterling."

(ii) Kodali Sri Lakshmi Narayana, "Book of Sri Raja Vankatadri Naidu" Pag:257

36. G.Mackenzie – Kistna District Manual P.314 – "That is 1818 only two years afterward, the copper sheets were stripped off the roof of the palace at Amaravati and were despatched to Subnavis Antana Pantulu at Masulipatnam to defray legal expenses. Where all the money went, no one seemed to Know."

37. (i) Bharati episode, March 1936

(ii) E.MARSDEN 1902, Book History of India, Page 176.

38. A Manual of the Kurnool District Narahari Gopala Kristnamah Chetty Madras 1886 Page: 123 "Captain Newbold, writing in 1837, says that passing through the jungle near Pacharla, he observed a skull bleached by the sun dangling from the branch of a tamarind tree, which was informed was that of a murderer and hill robber put to death by the headman".

39. (i) In the Short Introduction to the Kolatapu song collected by Acharya Donappa, the Uyalwalwada Narasimhareddy incident dates back to 1800 and 1825.

(ii) This event took place from 1800 to 1825 (Triveni page. 270).

(iii) Civil Disturbances during the British Rule in India (1765 1857) S B Chaudhuri 1955, Page: 29,152

(iv) Manual of the Kurnool District Narahari Gopala Kristnamah Chetty Madras,1886 Page:42

40. Acharya Tangirala Venkatasubbarao, Renati Suryachandrulu. Armed Rebellion, Page: 141

41. (i) Dr. Tangirala Venkatasubbarao thesis Telugu epic poetry Bharati Essay.

(ii) Triveni Andhra Pradesh Folk Songs A.P. Published by Sangeet Natak Akademi, Hyderabad 1960. Pages: 270-71 (Song collected by Toomati Donappa)

42. Cuddapah district Manual (Page: 145) Narasimha Reddy was hanged at koilcoontla, and his body exposed in chains in a cage where the bones continue to this day (1875) as a warning to bad characters (Page: 145)

43. Vaddadi Subbarayudu, "Namanandana Satakam(1877)"

44. Life of Sir Arthur Cotton – By his daughter Lady Hope, Page:186-19

SKY WAVES

Though nature mostly nurtures us like our mother, it has its mood swings. It takes time to adjust from those mood swings, and that time could wreak havoc in human lives and show us our real place in this vast universe. The Pakanati society had to face such a time of upheaval in its relation with nature that season. It was the first-ever blow these agrarians faced where heaven and earth conspired against them and tossed them to the winds and rain. It was winter. The streets were going empty before dark. A sudden wind was threatening to blow out the lamps in the small shops that were still open. The shopkeepers and street vendors were running hither and thither to hold their merchandise from getting spoiled with the dust blowing. It was Deepavali season. The rain that has suddenly started was already spoiling the crackers that were kept for sale.

Farmers were looking at the sky, trying to assess when this rain would subside and if they can start seeding black gram crop the next day. Suddenly the birds and bats that were resting on the trees nearby flew away with loud noise as if sensing something untoward was coming that way. Looking at the continuing rain, people decided to go to bed early. The rain became a torrential downpour that was not subsiding. It was going to be the darkest night in the history of the region.

It was 11th November 1864, and about 11 pm that night, the Sea overflew, and the swell took the villages by surprise, inundated the areas within seconds with monster waves measuring as long as coconut trees. The deluge took everything with it into the Sea. The farm crops, the domestic animals, homes, public utilities, men, women, children.... everything was dragged into the sea womb. Nothing could last in front of those 15-meter-long waves. Over 30 thousand human lives were lost to the Sea that night, with over 8 lakh livestock too perishing in that nature's anger.

The rain had disappeared by the morning. The Sea also went back to its place by then. The sun also came up as was usual. But it was a morning of death for that entire area. "Bandaru Uppena" was one of the most dreaded incidents in the lives of the Pakanati people.

Thousands of tons of best quality teak kept in the Bandaru Port by the British to be shipped to England also got tossed into the Sea, some logs spreading too far and away[45]. Few seafarers worked, some of them catch teak logs and survive their own lives. Some of them came to Dokiparru with the teak wood and stayed at the inn in the village till 15th December 1864.

Village elders Polavarapu Hanumanthayya and Pamireddy Nagireddy worked on getting all the teak logs collected and stored at one place in the village. When the villagers saw all those teak logs in one place, they realized the extent of destruction the British are causing on the natural resources on their land. The villagers would be obstructed by the British when they try to cut trees in the nearby forests or the trees grown in the government lands. They would have to face police cases and severe legal actions, whereas the British were shipping loads and loads of teak logs to England, cutting the Nallamala forest.

The Cantonment of Kaja village was mostly destroyed in the sea swell. Few British soldiers who survived were shifted to Samarlakota Cantonment. Collector Thornhill arranged for medicines, clothes, and other necessities to be brought from ships travelling from the Arabian Sea, Sydney port, and Chennapatnam Port. The dogs and other wild animals would dig up the buried dead bodies. The British were hard-pressed for personnel to guard these mass graves against such attacks. Challapalli Raja, Yarlagadda Ankineedu's fort got damaged completely. Valluri Estate King usually held the Krishna District Abkari auction. Because thousands of toddy trees got uprooted, so many deaths in the area and the drastic reduction in the income of people, the Valluri King was not inclined to take the Abkari Contract that year. But he was convinced to take it after repeated requests and an offer for reduction of fees from Rupees 1,46,000 to 35,000 only [46].

The seawater that inundated the villages also spoiled the Kharif Paddy crop in the entire area. The saltwater led to the spread of cholera, dysentery and other infectious diseases. Due to lack of proper food, water and also these diseases, deaths continued in the villages. The Pakanati families could not think of leaving their new homes again due to this natural disaster. They decided to protect their homes and village no matter what. They set to work, taking measures like digging saltwater canals that would stop seawater from entering their fields, drinking water wells etc. They have started conducting village rituals like sacrifices to the River Goddess – Ganganamma every year.

By the year 1875, there were thirty Postal offices in the Krishna district. The Postal system was spreading far and wide in the country around that time. Mostly Bullock carts were used in transporting letters and other articles. Polavarapu Gangayya held the contract for postal transport from Peddakallepalli near Krishna River to Pallevada village near Kolleru. The route would go through Kuchipudi, Nidumolu, Dokiparru, Kavutaram villages to Pallevada. River Krishna flows northbound near the Shiva temple of Peddakallepudi village. People of the area believed that bathing here and seeking the blessings at Pallevada Shivalayam was equal to making the pilgrimage to Kashi. Mandali Krishnarao, who did a great service to the development of the Telugu language, was a Pallevada born.

The Railway line works in the Bombay Presidency, from Bombay to Delhi, Calcutta, was finished by 1877. The Station Masters would be given some amount as salary and rest in the form of gold coins during those early days. This gold was also collected from various Samsthana's as forced contributions [47]. The trains were strongly opposed by the general public in those days as there were several prejudices and superstitions against these smoke bellowing, loud, noisy, heavy machines. The noise from the trains was believed to be harmful to pregnant. The loss of livestock on the train tracks was another reason for opposition. The horse carriages, bullock cart owners were afraid that they would lose their livelihood.

Under the circumstances, a train line was also proposed between Machilipatnam and Bejawada. A Land survey was also conducted for the line, which was rumoured to go through Dokiparru village. The villagers put up a united front opposing the line and succeeded in pushing it three kilometres away.

The Sankranthi festival was a big occasion for celebrations that saw entire villages participate with great enthusiasm. Cockfights were a major attraction. Competition between bulls to pull heavy stones was another major event. The Kuchipudi society would conduct many plays throughout the festival days. Harijans were allowed to participate in the festivities, only without any shirt or upper vest on them. Their entry inside the temples was still not allowed. Though all the villagers behaved like part of the same large unit, there were several unseen codes, restrictions that divided them. The Niyogi's eat their meals in plantain leaves; the Vaidiki Brahmins would use only plates made from Sal leaves. The Pamireddy's would pray at the Shiva temple they built; the Polavarapu families went to Madana Gopala Swami temple. Village elders Veeramachineni would take one route, Polavarapu would suggest another. Village Munasabu Pamireddy would point to another way.

Dasu Sreeramulu

Sri Dasu Sriramulu

Sri Dasu Sreeramulu was a native of Alluru village in Char Mahal estate of Krishna district. Born a Brahmin in a Niyogi family, Sreeramulu was a respected scholar and teacher. Great scholar Chellapilla Venkata Shastri referred to Sreeramulu as the "Reincarnation of Poet Srinadha". He carried the honorary title "Lion of Spontaneous Poetry – Ashu Kavi Simham". He wrote books like "Andhra Veedhilo Brahmana Prashamsa," and "Telugu Nadu", etc., in verse. He was a teacher at Gudivada school in 1873. From there, he was transferred to "Kavutaram" school in 1874. The kids of Dokiparru had to go to Kavutaram village as there was no school in Dokiparru. When the elders of Dokiparru village met and requested Sreeramulu to establish a school in their village and run it, he accepted their request and promised to start in 1875 [48]. As per his instructions, the Dokiparru villagers built a school building using the wood that was gathered after the "Bandaru

Deluge". Three more wooden bridges were also built using the remaining wood.

After the school building was finished, Sreeramulu shifted to Dokiparru and stayed there for three years, till 1878, getting the school firmly established. Kids from all castes were allowed to study in the school. But S.C.; S.T. kids had to sit there without any shirt, as was the custom of those days.

Erukala caste people would wear only a loincloth on them during those days. Their specific duty was to observe the sunrise and sunset.

Master Sreeramulu would get an income of Rupees 1500 from the school. He wrote "Samvaranopakhyaanam", "Lakshmana Vilasam" while he was teaching at Dokiparru. After the "Madana Gopala Swami" temple was constructed (1860), he dedicated his Lakshmana Vilasam to the temple's deity. Meduri Lakshmanacharyulu was the temple's main priest (son of Venkatacharyulu) then [49].

"Lakshmana Vilasam" describes the ancestral history of Polavarapu Hanumanthayya. Polavarapu Narasimha Rao, a family member of Hanumanthayya, still has a handwritten copy of "Lakshmana Vilasam".

With the abundant grace of Dokipura Gopala,

   Son of Kannaya, Kamambika,

   Named Dasu Rama wrote this book

   With the aim of the wellbeing of the whole society …

--- Shri Dasu Sreeramulu

"Lakshmana Vilasam" has a beautiful description of washermen carrying palanquins.

As a palanquin carrier

   His shoulders have gone rough,

As a washerman, cleaning so many clothes,

   His hands have gone rough

… man with a French beard.

--- Shri Dasu Sreeramulu

Sreeramulu had also written many plays and got them played by the villagers under his supervision. While still working as a teacher, he finished his Law education [50] and shifted to Bandaru town to practice law. The villagers were so sad with his leaving them that to show their gratitude, they turned their gold jewellery into flower-shaped ornaments and showered them on him during his farewell. The villagers also gifted him a palanquin and carried him themselves in that palanquin out of the village. His son, Vishnu Rao, was born in Dokiparru village.

Among all his writings, the translation of "Devi Bhagavatam" is equal to all other writings together. He is said to have written this book within six months in a status of deep anguish after his daughter's untimely demise. Even Kavi Samrat Viswanatha Satyanarayana mentions this detail about "Devi Bhagavatam". A 7,500 poems length book of verse and prose, "Devi Bhagavatam" is a masterly work.

His son Vishnu Rao was also a scholar who had won Rupees 20 by the Madras Rajadhani College for an essay he wrote on Indian history in 1895 [51].

Tooth Powder packed in One Rupee Notes

This is an incident that happened in the mid-summer of the year 1880. As the sun was beating down fiercely that afternoon, most of the streets were empty. A street vendor selling tooth powder was tired, unable to find any takers for his product. He was looking for a little shade to rest for some time. He found a big tiled house with big Neem trees offering ample shade. A 40 odd years old widow was sitting in the front yard with a hand fan in her lap. The street vendor went to her and requested some water to quench his thirst. The lady brought a tumbler full of cool pot water and satisfied his need. As he was resting under the tree shade, the woman asked him his details, where he was coming from etc. After answering all her questions, he asked, "Ma'am, can you please give me any papers to make small packets of this tooth powder I am selling?"

The lady answered in the affirmative – "There are so many papers in our Chest, I have no use for them, you can take them if you want." Then the lady took him inside, opened the chest and stood aside. The chest was full of many One Rupee Bundles apart from many other articles. The street vendor was confused and asked the lady again, "Which papers did you mean?" The lady pointed towards the big sized one-rupee bundles and asked, "Won't these serve your purpose?" The vendor understood her ignorance, promptly took all the rupee bundles, thanked her profusely, and immediately escaped from the area.

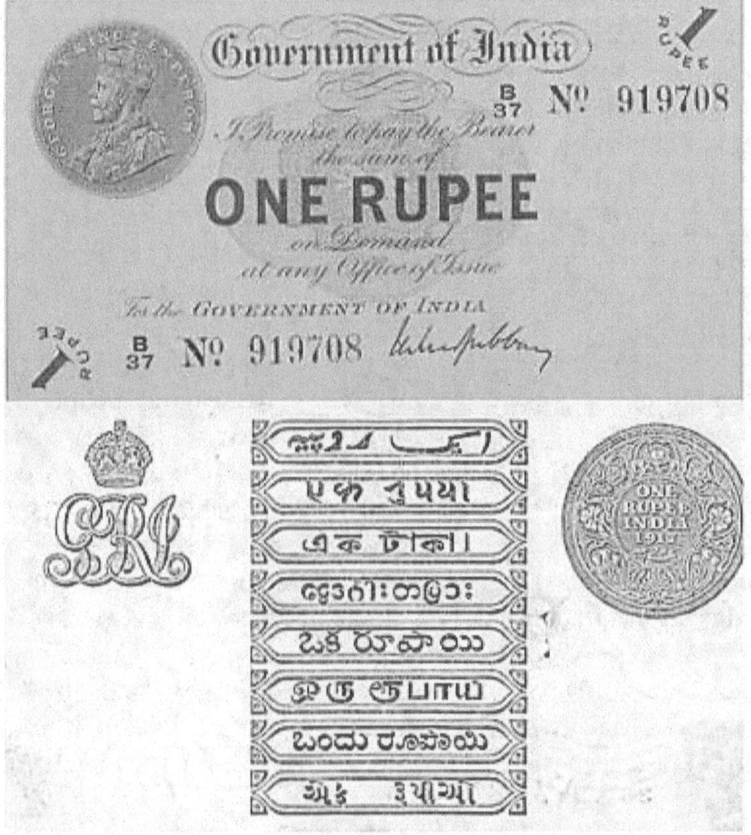

The widow's brother came the next day from the adjacent village to visit her. She mentioned that she got rid of some unnecessary papers yesterday by giving them to a tooth powder vendor during their conversation. The brother got alarmed, took her inside to show him those papers. When she opened the chest again, he saw few remaining one rupee notes and understood what happened. "Sister, this was a treasure your husband had amassed for you and kept safely here. You lost all of it due to your innocence," he blurted out, feeling sorry for the situation.

Such was the condition of women of those times. They were kept so far from worldly affairs that they wouldn't even know the difference between waste paper and cash. Her husband earned so much for her but never bothered to educate her in these basic things, which led to such a shameful situation. That too, she is a lady from the respectable family of great actor Chitturu Nagayya!

Motarfa Tax/ Tax on Head

The British were very particular about tax collection. When Samsthana's/ villages had more dues accumulating, they would depute special tax collectors, who were nothing but goons who would forcefully collect the dues from the farmers. Every village administration would vary the visits of these special collectors and would consider it a shame to the village and their administration if such demeaning people had to visit their village. Dokiparru Munasabu Pamireddy SambiReddy

Tax item (per head)	Rs.	A	Ps.
Barbers	2	5	8
Blacksmiths	2	5	8
Carpenters	2	5	8
Toddy workers	0	9	5
Washer men	2	5	8
Cobblers (Madiga)	2	5	8
Mala	0	14	2
Two-wheeled cart	2	5	8

would constantly remind the villagers of these "Mustakapollu" during the time of tax collection. But the village seldom went behind in paying their due taxes. Because of the congenial weather and the hard work they all put in, the crops would be good. The village Munasabu also had judiciary powers. He would sit in judgment during small disputes and petty crimes. The British had a "Motarfa Tax" or a "tax on every head"; tax on traditional caste-based occupations; even a tax on the salt the poor would use in their gruel.

The Turn for Vandematharam

In 1876, Governor-General Cornwallis introduced the Right to Land. It meant that the land could now be sold and bought by any other commercial commodity like any other commercial commodity. Dokiparru village also saw many such transactions taking place. Veeramachineni Venkata Krishna Rao bought an area of 500 acres and became one of the major landlords in the area.

The village school was running well, educating the youth of the region. The founder teacher Dasu Sreeramulu continued his advice to the school administration even after he shifted to Bandar and later to Eluru town. Village elders Pamireddy Ramashastrulu and Polavarapu Ramayya believed that educating the youth is equal to a continuous religious ritual and never reduced their focus on school affairs.

In 1891, Dasu Sreeramulu's son started a weekly called "Jnanodayam – Dawn of Wisdom" in Bejawada. In 1902 Konda Venkatappayya and Dasu Narayana Rao started "Krishna Patrika", which Venkatappayya edited.

In 1905, the division of Bengal by Viceroy Curzon caused great bloodshed across the country, which gave rise to the "Vande Mataram Movement." Bipin Chandra Pal, on a visit to Bejawada invited by Dasu Sreeramulu, spoke eloquently on "Swadeshi – Spiritual Freedom". Kavutaram, Dokiparru village youth worked as volunteers during that public meeting. Dokiparru's Pamireddy Ramashastrulu, Kavutaram's Bobba Padmanabhayya printed and distributed pamphlets titled "Vande Mataram – Manade Rajyam." The spread of these revolutionary ideas deep into villages alarmed the British and Anantapuram Collector Scott, known as a tough officer, was deputed suddenly in place of Krishna district collector Morriss to control the situation. Scott used the reserved police forces immediately, searching for activists across the villages. Luckily, the village youth were sharp enough to evade the police forces and disappear in the village.

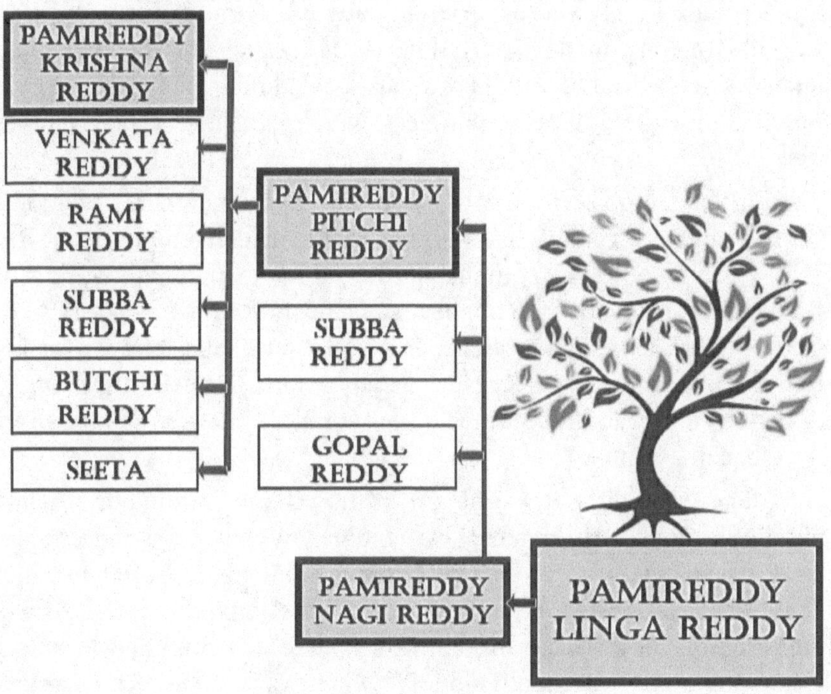

Pamireddy Nagireddy's eldest son was named "Pitchi Reddy" (Third Generation) after his ancestors. He was blessed with two more sons, whom he named Subbareddy and Gopalreddy. As the eldest son, Pitchi Reddy was very responsible and conscious about maintaining the family honour. He had a natural acumen for agriculture and enjoyed every activity related to farming. As a worldly-wise person, he would know about all the developments in paddy farming and focused on increasing the yield through better management systems, newer crop varieties every year. He would maintain his own seed bank and used to supply seeds too to interested persons. He managed to increase the family land pool to 65 acres from 30 acres. After the sudden demise of brother Subbareddy, he fixed up an allowance for his widow, distributed 35 acres to the other brother Gopalareddy and kept the remaining 30 for himself. "I find happiness in giving," he would constantly say!

Pitchi Reddy was married to Lakshmi (from the Manda family). They had five sons and one daughter. The eldest was Krishna Reddy (Fourth Generation). His siblings were Venkata Reddy, Rami Reddy (Ramayya), Subba Reddy, Bucchi Reddy and sister Seetha. Krishna Reddy was known for his moral rectitude. He would treat the entire village as his family and behave equally friendly with all. Rami Reddy and Subba Reddy were inseparable from eldest brother Krishna Reddy. Venkata Reddy was a fun-loving guy who would always be seen talking and making up tales. Krishna Reddy gave him the nickname "Pleader Venkata Reddy" as he was always talking. His talkativeness would also bring troubles sometimes, which Krishna Reddy had to handle.

In a combined family, one or two members wouldn't participate much in the daily work. It was not considered a big issue. But the family head would keep on pushing for all the members to work as it would increase productivity. Youngest son Bucchi Reddy studied B.A. in Gunturu Andhra Christian College. He was a rationalist known for his analytical view. Eldest son Krishna Reddy would have information of every activity of all family members but wouldn't interfere in any affair unless it became a must.

The drinking water problem in the village continued. Krishna Reddy would constantly make plans to dig new wells seeking enough drinking water supply to the entire village. Their plans would fail too, but they would start work on a new well without brooding much on the failure. Finally, they struck an abundant source of drinking water in a well they dug up in "Gummadi Doddi", which was named "Kanakamma Bavi."

Whose World Wars Are These?

"You reap what you sow". The First and Second World Wars happened entirely due to the political scheming of the British. The British are mentioned as a major force in world history, and India, as a British ally, gained nothing but loss of life and resources. All that remains of India's participation in World Wars is a list of dead soldier's names at the India Gate.

Indian Provinces contributed Rupees 900 Crores during the First World War, sent 14 lakhs army to the fight. Seventy-four thousand men lost their lives in the four-year war period. Britain gave an assurance of giving independence to India for assistance in the war, but the word was not kept. During the Second World War, too, Britain announced India's participation without even consulting.

After the First World War, England introduced a Dual system of Governance in 1919 to allay the pressure from the Indian public. Under the system, Central and regional Assemblies were established, with Indians electing members for them. These assemblies would take care of issues like agriculture, local Governance, health, education etc., while the British still hold key fields like finance, taxes, security and peacekeeping etc.

Marriages Turn Donation Drives for Libraries, News Papers

Sri Pamireddy Venkata Subbarao Reddy, who was the President of Krishna district's Farmer's Association, took part in the Library Movement also from the forefront. He eventually played an instrumental part in the establishment of the Dokiparru Library. He was an active participant in the freedom fight too. He would often say to his friends and relatives that he is ready to face any consequences, even jail or death. If it came to that, all he would expect is that the village supports his family. He inspired all his friends and villagers to donate all the cash gifts given to newlyweds during marriages to establish Dokiparru Library. An announcement in the "Zamin Raithu" paper on 26th May 1944 declares that inspired by Sri

Sri Pamireddy Venkata SubbaRao Reddy

Subbarao Reddy, Mr.Peketi Veera Reddy donated all the cash gifts that came during his daughter's marriage to "Zamindari" paper. Ramireddi Suryanarayana Reddy donated a building worth Rs. 4,500 to be converted as a choultry for public use.

During the freedom struggle, the general public mostly stayed away from tea consumption. The reason is that any amount that is paid for tea would reach the British coffers only, and taking part in benefitting the British were not encouraged by the public. Hence, they would stay away from tea consumption completely!

Zamindari Taxes

The Zamindars were the tax collectors from the farmers in the villages. The British would collect taxes from the Zamindars. After

Pithapuram Samsthan	Peshkash in Rs.	Income (Formar Tax)
1802	2,58,979.00	3,92,182.00
1874	2,58,979.00	5,51,231.00
1936	2,31,438.00	8,02,721.00

1936, the amount of taxes collected from the Zamindars by the British reduced in value, but the taxes collected by the Zamindars from the farmers increased multifold. The farmers looked at the Zamindari administration like leeches sucking their blood.

Name of the landlord	Peshkash In Rupees	Income (Farmar tax) In Rupees
Vizianagaram	4,66,464.00	20,90,394.00
Bobbili	83,446.00	8,33,000.00
Pithapuram	2,31,438.00	8,02,721.00
Polavaram	10,855.00	72,065.00
Challapalli	78,076.00	3,51,230.00
Muktyaala	17,511.00	78,882.00
Munagala	4,008.00	1,20,000.00
Venkatagiri	3,68,734.00	14,46,222.00

The Headaches of Zamindars

The Zamindars suddenly found their status reduced from rulers to the ruled after 1936 due to the removal of the Zamindari system. They were no more above the public. They were finding it hard to mingle with the general public. But the new social realities necessitated that they change their status. In their efforts in that direction, they made films like "Raithu Bidda", "Mala Pilla" and tried to say that they have reformed. They started posing like patrons of newspapers and literature [52].

In similar efforts, Challapalli Zamindar gave a big donation to the village library. He promised to donate a sixty-acre stretch of land near the Bhadra Reddy Lake for a school. The ecstatic villagers collected donations and organized for a thanksgiving meeting. The big-hearted Zamindar was taken on an elephant back in a massive procession to the meeting. All the speakers appreciated the magnanimous gesture of the Zamindar Sahab. But, alas, the Zamindar failed to keep his word at the end!

Just beside this 60-acre land bit, Cherukuri Ramayya had farmland of four acres extent. However, they would have constant boundary issues with the Zamindar. They were so vexed with the repeated headaches that they sold the land and shifted their family to Pedda Parupudi village near Gudivada. Cherukuri Venkata Ramayya is the grandfather of present media baron, publisher of Eenadu paper, Cherukuri Ramoji Rao!

Among the many Zamindars, very few could assimilate with the general public, and many others could not. Some others lost most of their riches, properties while attempting to adjust to the new way of life. They eventually lost their identities, some perished, and their names turned to dust in the cycle of time.

Five major reasons could be stated for such complete failures.

Arrogance

Arrogance is nothing but ignorance deep within one's soul. Very few Zamindars could conduct themselves with a sense of honour, respect and bonhomie with their subjects. With most others, the close circle employees like Karanam, Munasabu, Tahsildar gave the Zamindars and their families a wrong sense of importance and made them arrogant. Even the further generations also were filled with this arrogance and treated their fellow human beings like trash.

Sometimes these Zamindars would act so inhumanly that death punishment was issued even for small oversights. Such acts come from the arrogance that makes them believe that they are above all others. The accumulated arrogance in them overpowers their natural human instincts and leads them to commit atrocities. Chintapalli Venkatadri Nayudu's ghastly crime against the Chenchu's is an example of such a wrong sense of self and greed.

Indifference

Indifference is the result of fear and doubt taking over one's mind. The Zamindars would have so many issues to look into on a day to day basis. When there is an overflow of problems when solutions become hard to come, their minds would turn inwards, and they would show a strange indifference to all the problems surrounding them and behave as if there are no problems at all! This apathy might arise from lack of ability, the doubt that they are not strong or resourceful enough to find solutions. Because of the privileged life they led, some of them would not care to acquire any proper education, which would make their knowledge insufficient and anachronistic. Such closed minds would curl inside themselves when they face any problems instead of facing them and working towards solving them.

Such dearth in knowledge and analysis slowly resulted in them losing their wealth when the Zamindari system was abolished. Even when they faced a loss of wealth and social status, their indifference would not leave them, and their names perished slowly.

That is why indifferent persons would never win. Most of the times, they would criticize persons with the initiative as overzealous and greedy. But in reality, persons with initiative are good at analyzing situations. With this analysis, they would succeed in finding solutions that are not visible to others. Their readiness in trying those new solutions would bring them victory. "Victory favours the brave," as the saying goes. Indifference leads to defeat and death.

Fear

The Zamindars were always afraid of losing their wealth. People generally don't like losing money. Many times, people do not know how to address this fear of losing wealth. As this fear never left them, they usually resorted to amassing more wealth by increasing taxes on farmers. But undue, untimely increase in taxes would make them unpopular, which would result in further alienation from society. Thus they would continue losing. The secret about defeat is, it is actually an element of inspiration for victory.

But in their obsession to stay on top, the Zamindars pushed themselves into monetary issues often. To keep up the appearances, they would borrow. The many legal disputes would also drain their resources further and further. In fear of losing wealth, they would stubbornly try to preserve their property, getting more and more entangled in disputes, rather than be pragmatic and take up a route of compromise. In this fear of failure, they would further pressurize their young into being paranoid.

Laziness

Though the Zamindars appeared to be busy always, they were a lazy lot who always looked at evading their duties. They would spend time in literary activity, fishing, and resting in nearby islands, mostly doing everything other than what they should be doing. They would avoid acting upon serious issues, repeating maxims like "It is better to delay than to err." The human mind is generally endowed with the spirit for action. But when a person gets habituated to laziness, it leads to a struggle in mind. The conflict leads to anguish, distress and defeatism. This lazy and defeatist person loses all interest in proactive behaviour. Such persons become a burden on society. The older generations of Zamindari are unwittingly killed the instincts of their wards due to their lack of knowledge and perception of realities around them.

Bad Habits

Habits become the way of life for many before they could realize. Habits influence life more than education and values. Zamindars had a natural habit of rejecting everybody around them. When a person has no habit of listening to others, he would often miss positive advice. A prisoner to his habits, the person cannot escape. That is why, being unwatchful of the habits becoming a routine, a person stops accepting new thoughts. My ancestry and my pride are the bad habits that dragged these Zamindari progeny down.

References

45. Andhra Bhoomi, "Tatalanati Bandaru Uppena Katha," page: 252
46. Andhra Bhoomi, "Tatalanati Bandaru Uppena Katha," page: 255
47. Vasireddy Durgasadasiveshwara Prasad, Trains of India.
48. Dr. Velagapudi Vaidehi, *Siddantha Grandham*, "Works of Mahakavi Sri Dasa Sriramulugari", a review. Page: 6,335
49. Interview with Meduri Srinivasacharya.
50. Dr. Velagapudi Vaidehi, *Siddantha Grandham*, "A review of the works of Mahakavi Sri Dasa Sriramulu. Pages: 338,342
51. (i) Some pages of the genealogy written by Dasa Vishnurao, in print, are available from Sri Digavavalli Ramachandra Rao.
    (ii) Modern Andhra Shastra Maniratnalu, page: 90.
52. The book "Mana Zamindaru" by Sri Gorripati Venkata Subbaya (1944)

SWARAJYA IS MY BIRTHRIGHT

Sri Bal Gangadhar Tilak

"Swarajya is my birthright, and I shall have it!" said Lokamanya Bala Gangadhar Tilak, which became the sole guidepost to the Indian Independence Struggle in the later period. He was called a radical by the British for his outspoken slogan. By starting the Ganesh Festivals as a cultural extravaganza, he brought the Indian public closer and helped build a spirit of unity in an organically way. In the year 1903, the Bombay State had an income of 60 lakhs from liquor. Tilak started a movement to ban it, telling people that it is bad for health. The British did not like losing the income, arrested Tilak in 1906, and exiled him on a six-year sentence on treason charges. Tilak said that he considers it an honour for giving him such a sentence for working against the British Crown as it means that he is truly working for Mother India as a patriot.

Telugu Land's Daughter in Law, Sarojini's Disobedience

"Never stay aside thinking that Nation, Nationality, and yourself are separate things. Whatever happens to the country happens to you also; if the Nation is a slave, you are too…" said Sarojini Naidu and went around the country repeating these words, pushing the public to join the freedom struggle. This poet, the fighter, was the first female president to the All India National Congress meetings at Kanpur. Daughter in law of the Pakanati clan, her husband Muthyala Govindarajulu Naidu was a Pakanati Balija, Army family member. As it was an inter-caste marriage, her father was obstructed from officiating her marriage. Kandukuri Veereshalingam took up the duties and gave away the bride. Their family migrated to the Nizam area, and Mr. Naidu worked as a doctor in the army there.

Sarojini Naidu with Gandhi during the Salt March on the shore of Dandi

The British government banned the sale of any books related to the history of the country's independence struggle. Sarojini Naidu personally went around the streets and sold these books in the act of direct disobedience. She spoke on all public stages exhorting the youth to participate in the struggle. Her poetry was also an instrument she used strongly in this cause.

Simon Go Back

As per section 84 of the Indian governance act, The Indian Statutory Commission headed by Sir John Simon came on a country tour in 1928 to observe constitutional reforms being followed. Indian freedom fighters gave a call of banning it, with the slogan, "Simon, Go back." When the Commission briefly halted at Bejawada en-route to Calcutta, municipal chairman Ayyadevara Kaleswara Rao sent a letter to Mr.Simon through RamiReddy Subba Reddy (Kaza). Subba Reddy delivered it to Simon dressed as a servant. When Simon opened the cover, he saw a bunch of papers with 'Simon, Go Back" written on all of them. Simon was angry and surprised at the audacity of giving such letters to him directly but could not say anything to the person in the guise of a servant [53]. Later he did mention the spirit of independence he observed across the country to the British authorities.

Play on Bhagath Singh

Dreaming is common to all. But very few make plans and implement them to achieve their dreams. The independence of the country is the result of the dreams and hard work of many. Dokiparru villagers Polavarapu Ramarao, Polavarapu Gopala Krishnayya, Kanumuri Ramireddy, and Pamireddy Shesha Reddy organized a play on the life of Bhagath Singh by Vadali Village Drama Society. It was a dramatic interpretation, mainly with many events from Bhagath Singh's life and other incidents that were happening all around.

Sri Bhagat Singh

Bhagath Singh wanted to change the way the freedom struggle was progressing at that point in time. They planned for an incident that would shock the entire country and also the British administration. The idea was to blast bombs inside the Central Legislative Assembly in Delhi. The plan was not to cause any loss of life but to shock the administration and register protest against certain British Acts. Accordingly, Bhagath Singh and his friend Batukeshwar Dutt hurled two small bombs inside the assembly, threw pamphlets into the public from the gallery, and raised slogans against the British, before letting the police arrest them.

The British tried them for treason and presented concocted evidence to show them as terrorists who planned for major blasts to kill British officers. They showed evidence that over 7 thousand bombs were being made. Hundreds were arrested in relation.

Sri Kanumuri Ramireddy

On the 7th October 1930, Bhagath Singh, Raj Guru, and Sukhdev were sentenced to death by hanging. Despite the countrywide requests for the pardon of the young revolutionaries, the British did not spare them.

The play showed all these incidents, ending with the hanging of the trio. Bhagath Singh's character would hold a fistful of soil near the gallows and proclaim, "This fistful soil would influence the entire world" before getting hanged, bringing down the curtains.

Sri Polavarapu RamaRao

The British convicted Bhagath Singh in unfair judicial practices, hanged him secretly, and secretly performed his last rites.

The Vadali Drama Society's play was a big success. Every scene was movingly portrayed and performed by the actors. It became a sensation in the area. The authorities promptly arrested organizers Polavarapu Ramarao[54], Polavarapu Gopala Krishnayya for inciting unrest in the society. Kanumuri RamiReddy and Pamireddy Shesha Reddy were also arrested for helping and providing facilities to the Drama Society. They were sent to Rajamundry, Allipuram Jails.

Shabhash Andhra!

Sri Peketi RangaReddy

Between 1930 and 1940, many changes took place concerning the Telugu people within the Nation and outside also. These ten years are generally referred to as the "Hungry Thirties." The Tax Resistance went on in full swing in the Gunturu district. The police beat up Peketi Rangareddy (Kaza) in 1932 in a Lathi charge during a procession[55]. Hundreds of Munasabs resigned from their jobs. Vadali village Munasab Manda SeethaRamiReddy was among the very first to resign and stand as an example.

Dokiparru's Pamireddy Venkata Subbarao Reddy was the Krishna District Farmers Association president, while Nimmagadda Venkata Krishanrao was the secretary. Gandhiji went over Bandar, Dokiparru, Nidumolu, China Muktevi, and Challapalli on 14th April 1929 during a donation drive. Gottipati Brahmayya, Kanumuri Venkata Krishna Reddy took part in this drive along with Nimmagadda Venkata Krishna Rao. They kept a detailed, authentic record of all the freedom fighters from that area in the future too, and worked in making sure that they all got central government's pensions.

We Will, Make Our Own Salt

As part of the Civil Disobedience and tax resistance campaigns, Gandhiji gave this call "we make our own Salt." It started on the 12th of March, 1930, from Sabarmati Ashram to Dandi village on the Gujarath sea coast. It went on for 34 days. Similar marches were organized across the country, with

Sri Nimmagadda Venkata KrishnaRao

one in Krishna district from Dokiparru to Hamsala Deevi (where Krishna river merged with the sea), which was 55 kilometres away. Dokiparru's Nimmagadda Venkata Krishna Rao, who was the district Congress president, called for it [56]. The police held up Krishna Rao at Bandar crossroads. He was beaten with a whip 40 times and was left in the ditch beside the road in an unconscious condition. The farmers of Tarakaturu village rescued him the next day and took him to the hospital [57].

Committed Warrior

Pamireddy Venkata Subbarao Reddy of Dokiparru was a true patriot. As the district farmer's society president, he knew all the farmers and youth of the villages. With his extensive public access, he worked untiringly to spread the need and call for freedom struggle. "My troubles are but temporary. They would serve as warnings and examples to all the patriots fighting for the country," he would often say. He brought multitudes of village youth into the struggle. He underwent two years of rigorous imprisonment in Rajamundry and Ballary prisons. During that period, the police went to the extent of breaking down his house's doors and taking the pieces with him. His mother, Nagamma's anklets, were forcibly broken and grabbed. His mother's sister Macimma, who was visiting them then, was also threatened and was forced to give away her gold ornaments. The family's 18 acres of fertile land was entirely lost in court litigations attending to all the cases that were dumped on him for his activities during the freedom struggle [58].

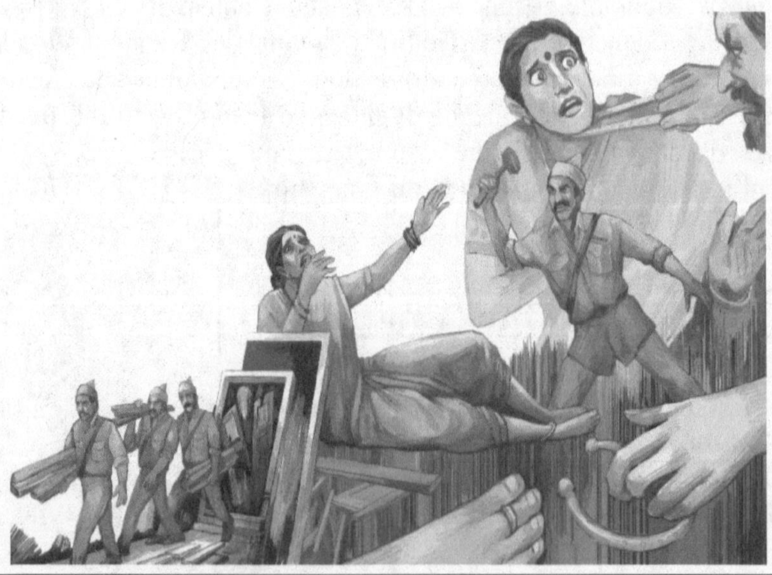

Perhaps the God troubles only those who can handle it. Village sarpanch Kanumuri Venkata Krishna Reddy, panchayat member Pamireddy Krishna Reddy took care of their family during those troubled times. Their family was forced into a situation where they had to live under a tree for over three months. But the family never complained, neither went back on doing what they believed in.

***

Objections against Colloquial Language

Around the year 1907, the language was entirely book-based official language. All the writing works were usually overseen by traditional Niyogi Brahmins. This official language had many strict rules and customs that were to be followed. It would not recognize any local dialectical usages; all grammar rules are to be followed without fail. If one thinks about writing in pure Telugu, one would have to be acquainted with rural language that had no connection whatsoever with Sanskrit education or literature. But such attempts were not encouraged by the aficionados of the language. They used all attempts at pushing back the usage of colloquial language and continue with the official language.

"Have you been to the Barampuram area, lad? Look at your language, utterly barbaric! Stand up on the bench! Or, a Hundred pushups! Or, Lean onto the wall on your knees…" the strict teacher would say!

Language of general usage is our actual mother tongue. It is the language of our place of birth, part of the regional dialect, with all specificities of the limited area, full of local jargon, anecdotes, and sarcasm, the colloquial language. Gurajada's **Kanyashulkam**, written in a colloquial language in 1892, was allowed to be read by the traditional Brahmins in their homes but not allowed to be taught at schools till about 1909.

People say, "Bends in the wood are dealt with by the fire." Just like that, the preference for colloquial language in Gidugu Venkata Ramamurthy Pantulu's heart was taking a stronghold. Subsequently, he took it up as a movement and started campaigning for it on all occasions. Mass movements like the freedom struggle also necessitated that all the public, with or without proper education, are brought in. So the movement for the usage of colloquial language took steam. Language itself has to include all the changes that time brings to it.

Language has to flow like a river for it to live on. Any attempts at restricting it to specific rules will kill it. **"Malapalli"** novel, written by Unnava Lakshmi Narayana during his jail term, brought acceptance to colloquial language from the traditional Brahmins [59].

In 1921, the right to vote was only limited to people who were paying at least Rs.10 taxes per year to the government. Hence there were

Dr. B.R Ambedkar

very few voters from rural areas. By 1926, due to increased water resources, transport facilities, and railway lines; conditions for famine went down significantly. These better conditions also resulted in the increase of land rates in the Krishna district from about Rs.40.00 per acre to around Rs.15,000 per acre. Even the per capita income also increased two and a half folds.

Earlier, the British preferred to keep the public separated based on caste for their administrative needs. Even the census was also done based on caste and religion. From 1921, the mention of caste from the census was removed[60]. The village-level courts were removed, with only district courts remaining, rendering the judicial recourse for the village public pushed away. Many other laws and rules were brought in that made life tough for the rural public. How can the British claim themselves as better administrators with such alienating measures?

It is nothing but the crooked British thought process which always wanted to keep the public separated as they would be difficult to handle if they were united.

Ambedkar's War with Untouchability

The Simon Commission toured across India in 1928 to observe the constitutional reforms that needed to be taken up. Following that, three round table meetings were held in London in 1930, 31, and 32. Gandhiji felt that he should be considered the representative of Harijans in the first meeting. Ambedkar opposed it. The British also did not accept Gandhiji's claim. Gandhi boycotted the meeting[61]. Ambedkar attended this first meeting as a representative of the Harijans, where he spoke entirely about the independence of the country and refrained from any reference to Harijan issues. The London press was thoroughly impressed with his oratorical skills and showered praises on him in their reportage.

According to him, the status of lone representative of the Indian freedom struggle did not go well with Gandhi.

The next year, Gandhi wrote a letter confirming his attendance at the next round table meeting. Ambedkar was to attend as a mere Harijan representative. Gandhi fell for the trap laid by the British here, which he did not realize. In the second meeting, while Gandhiji spoke in general, Ambedkar argued for Harijan rights and improvement in their conditions. He proposed a special reservation of constituencies for Harijans where their population is high. Gandhi opposed such reservations strongly, said that such reservations would break the Indian society. The Caste System is Indian society's special organization; following the caste-based occupations removes unnecessary competition between communities and is the secret behind the egalitarian economy in India, he argued.

In Gandhiji's view, service to Harijans is a religious obligation. Gandhi named the communities "Harijans" to reduce the social stigma attached to them. But Ambedkar argued for the abolition of the caste system entirely. He was dead against the evil of untouchability. He opposed Gandhi's ideas in this regard completely. He said that unless the untouchables are emancipated from their poverty, their social conditions would not improve. Political representation would create conditions for this, he declared. Gandhiji realized that he has been trapped by the British. Unable to openly oppose Ambedkar's proposals, which might have alienated the Harijans from him and the Congress, he expressed displeasure and walked out of the meeting. This is where the differences between Gandhiji and Ambedkar deepened. He termed it an insult to Congress. But it was a personal insult to him. The Congress entirely stayed away from the third round of meetings.

After the third round table meetings, the British announced Communal Award, which reserved constituencies to Harijans. Because his opinions were not honoured, Gandhiji went on a hunger strike in Erawada Jail, where he was placed at that point of time.

"Mahatma's come and go, but the untouchables are remaining untouchables," said Ambedkar during this fight for political relevance for the downtrodden communities. Though he was alone in this fight, he convinced the entire world with his arguments and perseverance. Due to his efforts, the reservation of constituencies for SC's and ST's started in India.

After waiting for some time, Gandhiji and his followers took revenge against Ambedkar by working against him during the 1946 Central Province elections and causing his defeat. Ambedkar fought in the by-elections for West Bengal's Jessore and Khulna constituencies and won. But the Congress acrimony with Ambedkar continued and when the time came, 52% Hindu district, Khulna; Chittagong hill region, and Chittagong Port Town were merged into East Pakistan, just because they were represented by Ambedkar [62].

Gandhiji never really tolerated any opposition to his opinions. He never really gave any value to the opinions or arguments of others. This is nothing but a sign of dictatorial mentality. Ambedkar was disgraced many times due to this. Any insults he faced were just impediments in his path for better India. But he always stuck to his goals and changed his approach according to the needs. Going ahead in this path, he wrote the Indian Constitution that is the backbone of our democracy.

Superiority due to birth

In a book on characteristics of poetry (Lakshana Grandham), writer Appa Kavi declares that a poet should be a god on the earth/ Brahmin, a peaceful person, and also says that a non-Brahmin is not eligible to write poetry. Chellapilla Venkata Shastri, in an essay titled "Kavitvam Brahmanatvam," states emphatically that poetry is entitled to Brahmins only. Tripuraneni Ramaswami Chaudhari, who had the sobriquet "Kavi Raju", did his barrister course at Ireland's Dublin and returned to India. to achieve social equality, he established "Sootha Ashramam" in Angalooru. This highly principled man was called a Brahmin hater by the general public. The world doesn't always like what you say, even if it is true!

In 1910, at Krishna district's Kavutaram, Kanthamneni Venkata Rangayya, Bobba Padmanabhayya conducted the very first Kamma caste congregation. The trend of caste meetings picked up and became fully established by the year 1917. Reddy Jana Sangh, Adi Andhra Society, Adi Velama Sangh, etc., mainly focused on demands for employment, more facilities in education, and other cultural support. In 1920, the Kamma's started their first newspaper from Bandar for the benefit of their caste. They started claiming that the Kamma's belong to Kshatriya's and not Shudra's. Acharya N.G Ranga, Gottipati Brahmayya, and others participated in the Kamma Society Meeting in 1926 at Bejawada [63].

Regardless of our desires, truth always gains prominence sooner or later. The notion that birth alone does not give any person precedence started gaining ground. People who accepted this point also started demanding the right to Veda's, to preach, and to conduct rituals in religious places. This became a movement in 1932. The Brahmin – Non-Brahmin opposition spilt onto the streets. Brahmins would say, "What crimes are the Brahmins committing? They are not Landlords; All that they have is their knowledge and education. Why grudge them?" But the opposition to Brahmins spread wide and deep in Krishna district.

The land tax-paying communities – Kamma's, Reddy's, Kapu's, and Velama's were counted as part of the Shudra's. All landlords were non-Brahmins only. They started conducting their rituals like marriages etc., in Telugu, refraining from using Sanskrit shlokas. "MalaPilla" movie under Gudavalli Ramabrahmam's direction, presented by Challapalli Jamindar, based on a Chalam story released around this time.

Does God belong only to a select few?

The rest house near the Dokiparru Shiva Temple was shifted by 1935 to Gudlavalleru varpu road and became Pakanati rest house. This was the main shelter for freedom fighters from Angalooru, Kautavaram, Dokiparru villages in the latter days. This became a centre for secret meetings. Erneni Subrahmanyam started "Gandhiji Ashram" and "Daridra Narayana" weekly magazine in Angalooru [64]. Mallikarjuna Gupta donated his entire property to this ashram. Potti Shree Ramulu also joined this Ashram in 1939, appreciating the Ahimsa principle of the ashram. Mallikarjuna Gupta, who was already there, was an old friend of Shree Ramulu. Under the Harijan Emancipation Movement, Shree Ramulu personally oversaw that Dokiparru's Agasteshvara Shiva Temple passed the motion to allow entry to Harijans. This motion was

Sri Pamireddy Ghantaa Reddy

implemented by Pamireddy Ghanta Reddy [65]. Persons who were deeply involved with all the affairs of the society only can change the society, and break the caste barriers, believed poet Jashuva. Declaring his belief, he wrote like this…

The Supreme God who assured his coming back

Whenever needed to establish Order on earth;

Did nothing really great on his previous visits,

Won't be a big difference if he didn't come now…

--- Jashuva

The Election Schemes

M.N Roy toured the entire Andhra area in 1937, sowing and spreading the seeds of rationalism. Many others took inspiration from

Sri Kanumuri Venkata Krishna Reddy

him and started movements with the same principles [66]. Those who understand the changing rules of life in every age act as torchbearers for change in society. The village elders believed strongly that education is a must to bring qualitative changes in the youth of Dokiparru and started making plans to support it.

In 1937, elections for the State Assembly also took place. It was a heated election environment across the country. In 1937, the right to vote was not extended to all the public. A person had to have 80 pounds or a100 rupees for him to be eligible to vote. The election officer would permit a person to vote if he is carrying a 100 rupees note; otherwise, his claim would be rejected. The village poor would be so far from voting under the circumstances. In the cumulative voting system, a person was allowed two votes which can be cast to the same contestant or different contestants [67]. Usually, the entire Dokiparru village votes would be cast to the Congress party. But this time, the voters cast one vote to Congress, and in place of the other, a request for sanctioning a school was added. This was widely covered in the newspapers. After the results were declared, the Congress government was established.

The media coverage of the Dokiparru voting helped in generating political interest in the village. Subsequently, village sarpanch Kanumuri Venkata Krishna Reddy met the minister Bejawada Gopala Reddy and got the sanctions for the second Government school in the entire Krishna district to Dokiparru in 1947. The dream and planning of Polavarapu Narasimha Rao finally became a reality. This was a big boost to the morale of the village elders.

Narayana... Narayana...

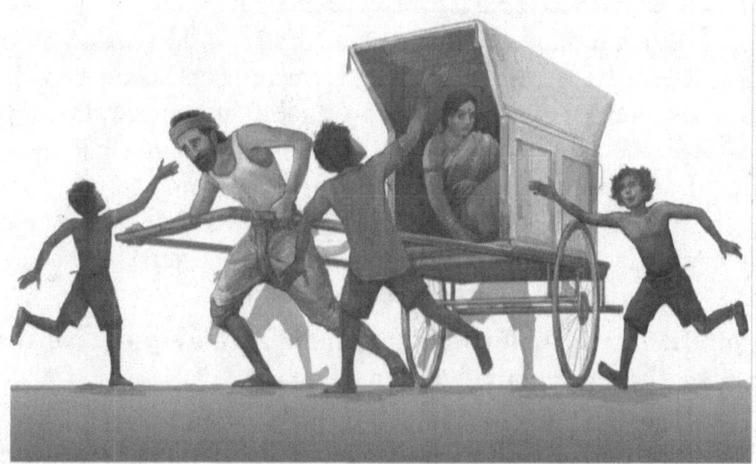

The Rickshaws, pulled by people, came to Machili Patnam in the year 1940. But there were hardly any takers for this new mode of transport. The reason was that children would run along with the rickshaw, almost the entire length, making fun of these people who wouldn't walk and were sitting in the rickshaw Their fun song equated them to persons without legs, making them embarrassed and abandon the journey.

***

The Madness of the Second World War

By early 1942, the clouds of war were already looming over the Indian horizon. Japan dropped few bombs on Vishakhapatnam and Kakinada, causing loss of property and few lives. There were rumours that Madras might be targeted next, and panic spread all around. The shooting of the film "Bhakta Potana" was halted for few months due to these rumours.

Hitler's warmongering turned Germany into a rabid nation hungry for violence. Hitler's hunger for land was insatiable as if he had a hundred mouths and thousand arms; he went on attacking country after country. Hitler's March towards Russia created panic in America and Britain too. Finally, Hitler perished, bringing an end to the Second World War. Indians suffered for a long time with the scarcity of necessities like food grains, paper, wood etc. The farmers took up the cause to make India self-reliant again by increasing food grain production by irrigating more lands, bringing more water sources into use by refurbishing old lakes and digging new ones.

Independence within a week?

When it thunders, light comes first, and then sound follows. In August 1942, "The Quit India" movement was announced all of a sudden. In the Bombay meeting, Gandhiji addressed the Congress Committee members like this: "I demand freedom right away, this night… I am not going to be satisfied with anything short of complete freedom… I say, 'Nothing less than freedom'… Here is a mantra, a short one, that I give you. Imprint it on your hearts so that in every breath, you give expression to it. The mantra is:

'Do or Die'. "We shall either free India or die trying; we shall not live to see the perpetuation of our slavery."

The intensity of Gandhiji's propositions created widespread fervour in the country. Vallabh Bhai Patel felt that this will push England to declare independence within a week! But it was not to be. The British administration cracked down on the movement like never before. Over ten thousand leaders were arrested within the night. Gandhiji was held in Pune's Aga Khan Palace.

Due to this heavy suppression, the coordination of the movement suffered, which resulted in incidents of violence at few places. The Quit India Movement has halted abruptly, despite support from foreign forces like America.

Chakravarthi Rajagopala Chari said that he would not support the Quit India Movement [68] and added that even if the British gave India independence now, in all probability, Indians might not be able to hold this independence. His comments drew widespread anger and heartburn.

Minister in the British government, Stafford Cripps, brought forward the proposal to bifurcate India. Rajagopala Chari supported this proposal and pressurized Gandhi to accept it. **"It is a post-dated cheque on a crashing bank,"** commented Gandhi before rejecting the Cripps proposal.

Azad Hind Fauj

"Give me your blood; I will give you freedom," this call by Subhash Chandra Bose made millions of Indian youth root for him. He was given the title "Nethaji."

Bose was an ICS who resigned to his position and dedicated himself to the freedom struggle. He believed that only the arms struggle would bring freedom to India. Not only believed it, but he also spent all

Sri Subash Chandra Bose

his life realizing the dream of independence his way. He was elected twice as the president of the Indian National Congress. He truly believed that Gandhi's Ahimsa could not be the only route to India's freedom. He was imprisoned by the British ten times. In the elections for INC's president post at Tripura in 1939, he defeated Gandhi's candidate Bhogaraju Pattabhi Seetharamayya by 205 votes. Gandhiji openly said that Pattabhi's defeat was his defeat.

The Second World War started in the year 1939. Bose felt that it is the right time to pressurize the British. He toured Russia, Germany, and Japan, seeking support to form an alliance against the British. With the support of Japan, he recruited India's War Prisoners and Malaya's (Malaysia) rubber plantation labour to form the army that he named the 'Azad Hind Fauj." It was formed in present-day Singapore.

He formed a Provisional Government of Free India also, declaring himself as the president over the radio. His government was recognized by Japan, Germany, Italy, and six other countries.

Japan gave control over the Andaman and Nicobar Islands to Bose. He named the Andaman Islands Shaheed Islands and the Nicobar

Islands Swarajya Islands. Due to insufficient support from Japan, Azad Hind Fauj failed in many of the tasks it took up. After the British Army defeated Japanese forces and Indian National Army, Bose tried to went and reach Russia to restart his campaign. He was reported missing with his plane crashing en route. The INA and the dreams it spread were shattered abruptly. But the widespread acceptance Subhash Chandra Bose and his INA received across India has drastically reduced the image of the British Army, which the British also understood.

Azadi in the village

Lella Sharabandi Raju from Dokiparru and Mohammad Hanif from Kaja villages joined Azad Hind Fauj and participated in the fight

Sri Lella Sharabandi Raju

against the British[69]. Mr. Raju worked as the Record Assistant in Dokiparru High School in the latter days. He would always read Ramayana and Maha Bharata to the school children. He was also a spontaneous poet who had the knack of including daily happenings quite easily in his poetry. He introduced Jashuva's poetry to the school kids. After his retirement, he contested the village sarpanch elections as an independent and conducted his campaign focusing on the importance of fair elections in a democracy. He had the equanimity to treat both victory and defeat likewise in him. He would always participate in the village affairs, helping whoever was in need.

Remembering her husband...

A person's greatness is forever. This is about one such great soul. Vidiyala Kalahasthi Lingam of Dokiparru village was an active participant in the freedom struggle[70]. He married Veeramma in the year 1930. He was an underground activist for many years, who was watched by the British always. He would still slip the British police and go to the designated place to pass the information needed. If he felt that he was being followed, he would hide under the big chicken coops that almost all householders used in those days. He would stay there for a long time, till he was sure that the police

Sri Vidiyala Kalahasti Lingam

have gone, and then only he would come back to his house. His wife knew this secret, and sometimes she would carry food for him to those chicken coops directly.After the big gathering at Kavutaram train tracks, Lingam had to hide again under a chicken coop nearby. But this time, the police identified his presence, arrested him and threw him in jail. For quite some time, his whereabouts were not known either to the family or the villagers. His poor wife would go around the village, checking under the chicken coops, with food for him in her hands. The villagers felt very sorry for her plight. Her wait for her husband, her search for him, her anguish continued for a long time, with the painful scene bringing tears to the watching eyes always.

She would yell, "Why the entire country's affairs have become your affairs? I am searching for you so much, why don't you come for me, why can't I see my husband again…"

Lingam finally came back after two years of jail time. His wife was so happy; her joy knew no bounds, which the villagers fondly recalled again and again.

This is a small anecdote that explains the sufferings common Indians faced, the lack of basic rights, the oppression under the British administration. Kalahasthi Lingam was arrested again when he took part in the agitation against the sale of an arrack at Koneru centre in Bandar and was punished with flagging in Pamarru police station.

The prisoners of the time were detained in atrocious conditions. They were shackled, hardly any clothes were given to them, their diet was hardly sufficient, forced to do manual labour, even the drinking water was not clean[71]. Many prisoners suffered mental breakdowns due to the bad conditions they faced. Great mental strength was needed to endure these conditions.

A Prison within the Home

Gonnuru Sarreddy of Kaja was another dedicated freedom fighter. He was a daring, uncompromising fighter that would never go back from his goals. His house would be always busy with all the activists that used to hang out there, discussing, planning, and taking shelter. His wife Narayanamma was a mentally troubled person who was kept in one of the rooms under tight supervision. The doctors suggested that a change of place could be beneficial to her condition[72]. Sarreddy had no other go. He sold three acres from his property and bought 15 acres of land in Bodhan town of Nizam State. Then he relocated his family there and later

Sri Gonnuru Sarreddy

participated in the struggle against the Razakars and Nizam King. Thus, he became one of those rare freedom fighters who took part in the Nizam State's and also India's freedom fight.

Division of the Country – Rajaji's Scheme

As per Gandhiji's suggestions, Raja Gopala Chari designed a scheme and proposed it to Mohammad Jinnah (in June 1944). It was mostly on the lines of the Muslim League's 1940 Lahore resolutions. Maulana Azad opposed it [73].

In March 1947, Mountbatten became the Viceroy of India. He announced that parts of Bengal, Punjab, and Assam would be divided on the basis of religion and would become part of the new country to be made. This declaration in June 1947 that India would be broken into two was a shock to the entire country, but the topmost leadership accepted it as a necessary compromise. "Some decisions have to be accepted, even if they are not to our liking," said Gandhiji.

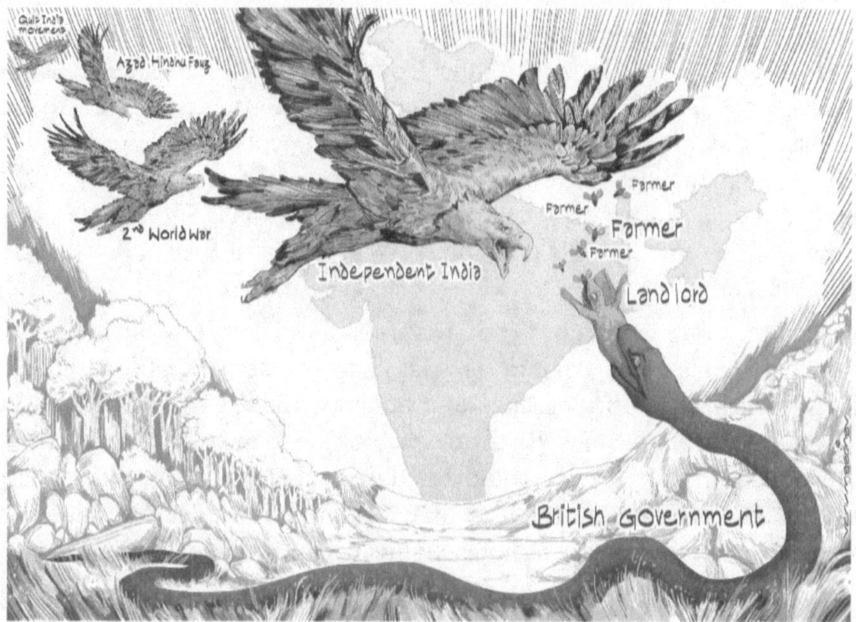

14th August 1947, as the clock turned into the 15th, the country became an independent nation. India's servility came to an end.

Rajaji's Shining Stains

Sri C.Rajagopalachari

Chakravarthi Raja Gopala Chari (1878 - 1972) was a Selam, Tamil Nadu advocate, writer, and politician. He was a known non-conformist. "Be very patient with your steps in politics," he would always tell his followers. He was an expert who used almost all his friendships for one or the other political ends. By marrying his daughter Lakshmi to Gandhiji's fourth son Devadas, he became a Gandhi family member. He was favourable to Muslim League's demand for a separate country and openly called for support for that proposal from major leaders of India; did all he could to complicate the division of Madras State. He was the major force behind keeping the Telugu people of nine taluqs of Madras district within Madras State forcibly. Due to his open opposition to the 1942s Quit India movement, the British complimented his administration of the Madras Presidency as the best in all Indian Presidencies.

Perhaps there is an element of King of Gods, Indra in Rajaji. Despite his open support to the bifurcation, and opposition to the Quit India Movement, he found a minister's portfolio in Nehru's first cabinet.

Moreover, when Governor-General Mountbatten got down, he was made the Governor-General of the Country. He was also elected the governor of Bengal after independence. He was also considered to be the first president of the country, but his comments opposing the Quit India movement may have cost him this seat. Earlier, his displeasure with the then collector of Selam district, a Telugu man, Shonthi Venkata Rama Murthi, cost him his position. F.W. Dickson, a British, was made collector there [74].

His comment that "The Andhra's do not follow up on their words" fomented the Andhra Special State movement and turned it violent. During the 58 long days of a hunger strike by Potti Sri Ramulu for separate Andhra State, Rajaji never took his name even once in the Madras Assembly! He once commented that scientists and engineers are unfit to enter legislative offices as they have no knowledge of politics or governance, as recalled by famous engineer K.L. Rao in his biography.

The Flow of Godavari

After entering the Eastern Ghats, up to about a forty-kilometre stretch, the river Godavari creates beautiful vistas with natural bends and valleys shaped by the hills in the region. Beautiful nature has enthralled many poets, writers; resulting in rapturous descriptions in many works of art. As the river enters the Ghats through Koida, Kondapudi, Tekuru, Kondamodalu agency villages, it bends, spreads or thins down according to the space offered by the hills, but keeps flowing. It is as if these Eastern Ghats are disciplining the unruly river! Near the 7 kilometre mark, after it enters the Ghats, the river passes through a narrow space of 656 feet only! At the height of 3,500 feet from above sea level, the villages offer abundant scenic beauty and rare indigenous culture and lifestyle.

Through these narrow passes, the river flows at a rate of 20 feet per second, 24 KM per hour. Geologists say that the sea was probably spread up to these Eastern Ghats in ancient times, hence the valleys are at 50 feet below sea levels even today. After 32 kilometres, near the hills at Polavaram, the river spreads up to 1.6 kilometres in width. Near the Rajamandry Railway Crossing, it further widens to 3.5 KMs, finally getting widest at 9 KMs near Dhavaleshwaram.

An American engineer with vast experience in constructing dams, Dr. J.L. Savage, surveying for the Sree Ramapada Sagar in 1947, opined that the "beauty and diversity of river Godavari in the Eastern Ghats is incomparable with even the most beautiful of American rivers."Arthur Cotton has also mentioned that the amount of water that flows in the Thames River in England in one year, is perhaps lesser than one day's flow of river Godavari in a surge.

Due to the South-West monsoon, Godavari during July – December is "Varada Godavari – Overflowing Godavari." Between January and July, it is "Pilla Godavari – Lean Godavari." Calculations tell us that the least amount of water flow in the Godavari was 930 T.M.C in 1920-21; whereas the highest was 33 lakh cusecs in 1953.

The mighty flow of Godavari during monsoons must be utilized properly for human needs, and the only method for this was to divert the water to other needy places. Dr. Shonthi Venkata Rama Murthy and Dr. K.L. Rao met Prime Minister Nehru and explained these details to him, requesting him to include the construction of reservoirs in the Five-Year Plans.

Due to his love for North India, Nehru felt the need for Hirakud, Bhakra Nangal, and Farakka projects as more immediate needs in comparison with Godavari projects. He sent K.L Rao to oversee the northern projects. Other north India leaders fomented the water disputes between the Southern States higher, getting their projects finished in the melee. The politics of those days created differences between leaders like Rajaji (Tamil Nadu) and Prakasham Pantulu (Andhra).

Dr. Shonthi Shree Ramamurthy's continued struggle

When India was dependent on imports of food grains from other countries due to famines, just 7% of Godavari water was being utilized properly, with the rest flowing into the sea. Dr. Shonthi Shree Rama Murthy, who was the Chief Secretary of the Madras State, fought for the construction of dams on the Godavari, for the welfare of Andhra State. He demanded the linking of Godavari with Krishna River in an essay he wrote in 1937 for Andhra Patrika. The Madras Presidency assigned engineer L. Venkata Krishna Ayyar for a survey.

Mr. Ayyar filed a report in 1941, suggesting that the area near Koida and Ippuru villages, about 50 KMs from Dhavaleshwaram, was the right place for the construction of a dam. He proposed slipway canals to divert the water using gravity.

The report was further discussed by K.L Rao and Shonthi Murthy [75]. In 1860, the Bhadrachalam region was made part of the Central Province and later merged with Madras Province by the Nizam to facilitate the construction of the dam. The dam to be built was to be named Rama Pada Sagar. For a better understanding of the geological conditions and the planning of the dam, American expert J.L. Savage was brought to India. Savage had already supervised the

Sri S.V Ramamurthy I.C.S

Parker Project in the Colorado State of America in the year 1939,   to increase food grain production there.

Creating a new hurdle, few people from the Madras Province sent a report to the Nizam, which said that the Singareni Mines of Hyderabad State would be submerged if the Rama Pada Sagar project is constructed. The Nizam government immediately objected to the project. Dr. Shonthi Rama Murthy had to personally visit ministers Nirja Ismail and Engineer Ali Navaz Jung in Hyderabad to explain and convince them that the Singareni Mines won't be affected by the dam construction. Even after his retirement, Mr. Murthy would go along with K.L. Rao to meet Prime Minister Nehru, Finance Minister John Mutthayya and inquire about the project's status. The Tamils sent a report again around this time that the project would cost about 120 crores with hardly enough returns. Rama Murthy sent his report countering such calculations. The progress in the project hit a roadblock.

Dr. Shonthi Rama Murthy contested the 1952 general elections from Rajamundry on behalf of Prakasham Panthulu's Praja Socialist party. He conducted his campaign with the major promise that his victory would clear the path for Polavaram Project. Due to rumours that he had withdrawn his candidature from the elections, Mr. Murthy lost. He explained these happenings in his autobiography "Looking Across Fifty Years." Dr. Sarvepalli Radha Krishnan wrote the foreword to another book, "Science and Spirit", written by Mr. Murthy.

Andhraits Troubles in the Arava State

"Mother is insanely rich, but the son is a pauper!" Constructing a reservoir at Telukutla near Gurajala to the Krishna river, and connect to the Pinakini with canals was the plan under Krishna Reservoir Project. But the Madras Presidency felt (in 1930) that a barrage on the Kaveri River at Mettur was an immediate need. Chief Minister P.

Subbarayan answering a question in the assembly, said, "We received proposals for two barrages; one was Mettur Kaveri project and the other Krishna Reservoir Project. Due to the availability of funds, we could take up only one. We took up Metturu Project." This was the kind of neglect Andhra region projects suffered under the common government.

Per the Telugu people's wishes, the Andhra Maha Sabhas between 1913–16 were conducted at Bapatla, Bejawada, Vishakhapatnam, Kakinada and Nellore. Indian National Congress also constituted a separate Congress Division and tried to control the demand for a separate state. In 1936, British India created Bihar and Orissa States. Telugu regions of North Ganjam, Jayapura were included in Orissa.

All the representatives from the Andhra region pressed for the formation of a separate Telugu State. Assembly speaker Bulusu Sambamurthy wanted to take a delegation to London to explain the necessity of a Telugu State to the British. But Chief Minister Rajaji was consistently working towards downgrading the demand for a separate state. Under his influence, Congress leadership declined permission to Sambamurthy's trip to London, leading to acrimony in Telugu representatives.

Rajaji always worked towards keeping his closeness to Gandhiji intact. He put a lot of effort to control people from reaching him. He would only send those leaders who would sing his greatness in front of Gandhiji and also those who would find fault with Andhra leaders.

In the Madras State Cabinet under Rajaji's leadership, Prakasham Pantulu handled the Revenue portfolio. The influence of Sanskrit on the Arava people of Madras is very limited. They are more influenced by the non-Brahmin movements of the time. But the influence of Sanskrit on Telugu is more. Like this, Tamil and Telugu are two distinct, different cultures. Even the thought process of the public is also different.

In 1938 March, the Madras Legislative Assembly and Council passed a resolution to have separate administrative zones for Tamil, Telugu, Kannada, and Malayalam regions. The PWD Minister started changing the village names, street names into Tamil script. Even the milestones on the highways were also being written in Tamil. Even Telugu majority towns and villages were also being converted/ changed to Tamil names. Chenna Patnam's well-known "Papayya Street", which was named after a famous Telugu person Papayya (1809), who was an expert Dubasi, was generally in Telugu and English on boards. His surname was "Avadhanamvaru." When proposals to rename this street came, due to strong opposition from Telugu people, an "r" was added to the name, making it "Papayyar Street" [76], sounding Tamil, yet continuing with almost the same name!

During Quit India Movement, when thousands of congress cadre was being jailed, Rajaji openly opposed it and later supported the idea of Pakistan too. Because of these steps, his popularity had gone down significantly. Maulana Azad removed him from Congress in 1942 and was forced to take him back into Congress just before the elections [77].

In 1946, when it was time to choose a person as Chief Ministerial candidate, the Andhra Provincial Congress Committee President Tanguturi Prakasham and Tamil Region Committee President Kamaraj Nadar, along with Kerala Congress Committee President K. Madhav Menon, went to see Gandhiji at Delhi's Bhangi Colony. His only words were, "You should have already selected Rajaji, do that! [78]"

Prakasham Pantulu was a seasoned politician who would tread all waters fearless of any depths. He put the issue to voting among the committee. Rajaji drew 38 votes in favour, while 148 were polled against! Thus Prakasham proved that the public did not support Gandhiji's opinion. Gandhi could not digest the defeat Rajaji faced here. He threw allegations of corruption against Prakasham Pantulu.

Gandhiji's allegations against Prakasham

Gandhiji wrote

"When I was travelling to Chenna Patnam from Orissa to attend Hindi Prachar Sabha's Silver Jubilee, while entering the Andhra region, State's Congress Secretary Mr. Kala Venkata Rao came to welcome me. I asked him, "How Prakasham is able to lead a public life while continuing as a lawyer?" He replied that "He stopped practising law and entirely living upon the public money."

After you came out of jail, when the public gave you huge amounts as contributions, people say that you did not deposit those amounts to the party, but used it all to your personal needs? This is gross corruption. You are not eligible to be in the assembly as a member or to be a leader in public life. I suggest you resign immediately."

Prakasham Panthulu's reply

"There are two ways for people in public life to lead their lives—one, when some rich man creates a fund in their name, using that money for subsistence. Two, when the person is in any need, the public comes forward to donate those funds. It may be contributions enough for a month or a year. The 50 thousand rupees I received recently was money donated to me by the public.

Sri Tanguturi Prakasam Pantulu

When I was charging a fee of a thousand rupees as a lawyer, then too, I treated that money like public money only. Whatever the way, the money used by a person in public life is public's money," replied Prakasham Panthulu.

His honesty did not need any special testimony; the holes on his clothes when he died were the silent proof!

Potti Sri Ramulu's Sacrifice

The Central Government of India constituted Linguistic Provinces Commission with SK Dhar, retired Allahabad High Court Justice, and others to look into the matter of reconstituting the Indian States based on languages. The Commission, while recommending the reconstitution of few states, did not support the linguistic reconstitution per se. Another committee, JVP Committee, with Jawaharlal Nehru, Vallabh Bhai Patel, and Pattabhi Seetha Ramayya as members was constituted, to discuss the recommendations of the Dhar Commission. The JVP Committee, too, in its 1949 report, felt that the time is not opportune for the creation of any new provinces.

In 1951, the Madras State government planned for a project on the Krishna – Penna Rivers, which would give 100 T.M.C to the Rayala Seema region and also supply water to nearby Tamil districts. The Planning Commission approval was also taken for this. Another project was also proposed by the State's Chief Minister Rajaji, to link Penna and Kaveri Rivers (1952) and was being planned which would ensure more water supply to the Tamil region. The Telugu people opposed these projects strongly and began a movement against them. On the 18th of October 1952, Potti Shree Ramulu started a fast till death, demanding an immediate formation of a separate Telugu state. CM Rajaji belittled

Sri Ramulu's purpose and dedication when it was brought up in the State Assembly. But Sri Ramulu's determination never faltered. It was day 50, day 52, day 54… all the streets of Chenna Patnam shook with fear for the great man and the repercussions of his daring act. Sri Ramulu passed away on the 58th day of fasting [79].

There was a national outcry over the death of this great personality. His body was brought on a bullock cart from Mailapur to the graveyard, with over a lakh people following in a procession. The anguish of the Telugu people knew no bounds. There were large spread protests and acts of violence at few places. It is perhaps wrong to say that Sri Ramulu died due to fasting. He died due to the apathy of the government that rejected the recommendations of many committees, public demands, and believed in the personal grudges and prejudices of individual leaders, rejecting this genuine demand. It was not his sacrifice; he was sacrificed to the personal egos and selfishness of certain politicians.

Sri Potti Sreeramulu

In October 1953, the Andhra State was formed. Rajaji felt that if the Andhra's are allowed to use Madras as a temporary capital, their strength might continue there, and he literally necked them out of Madras by the third day itself. The Telugu's who were lost in their happiness over the creation of their own state did not think much about several issues. They did not stress for an equanimous distribution of wealth. The Central Government assured that enough funds would be given to make Kurnool into a suitable capital, with the Madras State also giving financial support. But after the State of Andhra Pradesh was created in 1956 and the capital shifted to Hyderabad, the issue of funds and support were conveniently forgotten.

<u>Sanctity of Duty and Dedication</u>

As it was about 100 years since the construction of the Krishna Delta barrage at Bejawada, built by Arthur Cotton, the barrage and other structures were badly in need of repair and refurbishment. The earlier

Sri Vepa Krishnamurthy

Madras government did not care much for this work despite the many representations by farmers from this region. As was feared by the farmers, the 1952 floods to the Krishna River spoiled parts of the barrage, and some sections of the structure were lost in the flow. Chief Engineer Vepa Krishnamurthi tried to fill the breaches with bags of sand to protect the leak. Krishnamurthi and six others lost their lives in their valiant effort [80].

Inauguration	Krishna Delta works – 1852 Prakasam barrage – 1954
Water assignment	181.20 TMC
Barrage capacity strategy	3.071 TMC, 13.08 Lacks
The length of the main canal	East canal – 370 k.m. West canal – 322 k.m.
Estimated cost	Krishna Delta works 2 Crores (Dam and Construction of canals) Prakasam barrage 2.78 Crores (Dam construction cost)
Construction phase	Krishna Delta works completed in 1855 Prakasam barrage completed in 1957

Prakasham Panthulu got the repair works on the barrage started on an urgent basis, and a new one was built in place of the old. This one was named the Prakasham Barrage.

✳✳✳

Sports in the Villages, Schemes

"Daadi – Attack" is a village game. The game is a test to scheming and future planning of the players. Just like a chess game, this one also tests and teaches concentration, planning, analysis, and competitive spirit in the players. The players move their coins, killing the opponents' coins, yelling "daadi," exhorting, challenging the opponent to overpower him. This game teaches the skill to face problems and hurdles in life. Pamireddy Krishna Reddy used to play this game quite often with his brothers.

SWARAJYA IS MY BIRTHRIGHT

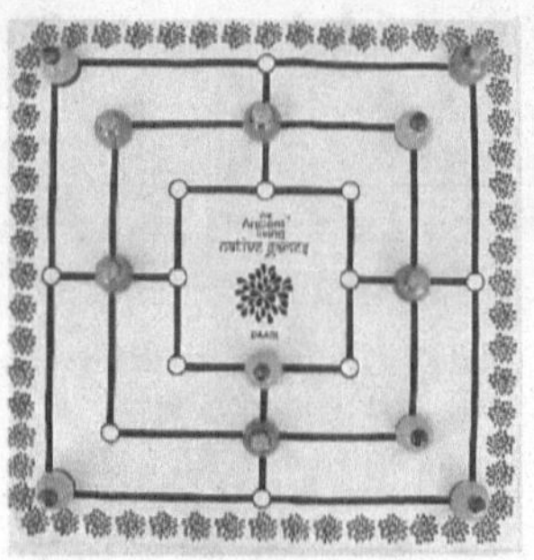

After Pitchi Reddy passed away, Krishna Reddy and his brothers divided their land six acres each. As the youngest, Butchi Reddy was just eight years old. Krishna Reddy took his responsibilities and brought him up with lots of love and care. By the time Butchi Reddy finished his B.A, Krishna Reddy had handed over his share of six acres with four acres added to it.

Their most trusted employee was "Gantayya", who was treated like any other family member. All the members of the family had their designated duties, with Krishna Reddy overseeing all. They preferred the usage of organic fertilizers over chemical fertilizers. As the import of Urea had already begun by then, most of the farming community started using it extensively, but Krishna Reddy insisted on traditional organic fertilizers. He urged fellow farmers also not to use the chemicals in their farming. When he was a member of the panchayat, he insisted on passing a resolution in favour of organic fertilizers. But as the majority of farmers preferred the easy route, the resolution was not implemented in full spirit.

Krishna Reddy insisted on marrying his brothers with girls from Pakanati families only, as was the custom. But his brother Butchi Reddy insisted on marrying an educated girl only. As there were no educated girls in Pakanati families, Krishna Reddy had no other go but to accept girls from other Reddy clans. The Pakanati's marrying other Reddy clan persons started this way.

When customs become compulsions, they become shackles that cause pain and friction. These forced customs turn natural, reasonable acts into big crimes. The older generations used to feel that moving out of their villages is a big punishment.

After his brother's marriage, Krishna Reddy decided to move to the Jamulapalli area as he felt that it is a more traditional town. This was perhaps destiny's design. Younger brothers Subba Reddy, Rami Reddy came to see off their elder brother. Subba Reddy recalled the incidents of the journey…

"We all reached the Kavutaram Railway Station to take the train to Jamulapalli. We waited to stand on top of the sand mound on the right side. It was about 8 AM. Many milk sellers were carrying milk to take to Bejawada, in big copper vessels with small lids. The train came from the west, making a loud noise, and stopped near the area we were waiting at. As we were carrying a lot of luggage, we ran ahead carrying one or two per head. The basket that was filled with rice, curries, and other eatables for the journey was carried by sister-in-law Bhadramma. Brother Krishna Reddy carried the big bag of clothes.

Younger brother, Butchi Reddy's friends, had come to help us with the luggage. They all ran ahead, carrying the luggage to the bogey. All of us could secure seats. The third-class bogeys were like long wooden boxes. Wooden benches were fixed facing each other. There were fans on the ceiling, but they were hardly supplying enough air in the heavily crowded box. The route was a single track only, so if any other train was coming from the other side, our train had to stop and wait aside in the station for long times. As they were steam engines, the speed of the train was very limited. They were releasing a lot of smoke.

By the time the train reached the Rajamundry Godavari Bridge, the driver had reduced the speed to the minimum. The water in the river was reddish. We could see people moving here and there on the sandbanks in between. There were cattle resting near the grassy knolls. The sun on the west side was a similar colour to the reddish water in the river. The train was rocking us like in a cradle. I took an anna coin from brother Ramayya and deposited it in the river.

Brother Ramayya was lost in his thoughts. Was he worried about elder brother Krishna Reddy going away from us? The train reached Pithapuram. A train journey of this length was a first for me and brother Rami Reddy. Three bullock carts were waiting for us at the station. The luggage was adjusted in all the carts. Then the journey to Jamulapalli started. The carts were going through picturesque fields. We finally reached Jamula Palli. All of us jumped into the Eleru River stream that was flowing beside us. After washing off all the dust from the long journey from our heads, we felt fresh and light. The stream water was very clear and sweet to drink."

The Nile River of Egypt is northbound. If we look at the history of the middle ages surrounding the Nile River Bay area, they had a belief that in areas of northbound rivers, people of great calibre with the capacity to change history are born. In India, too, temples with north-facing are considered powerful. Indians too, believe that miracles happen near water sources that are northbound. Near the Kashi

Vishvanath temple at Varanasi, the river Ganga flows north side. Krishna river near Shree Shailam's Mallikarjuna Swami temple also flows northbound. Eleru River flows northbound near Jamulapalli village.

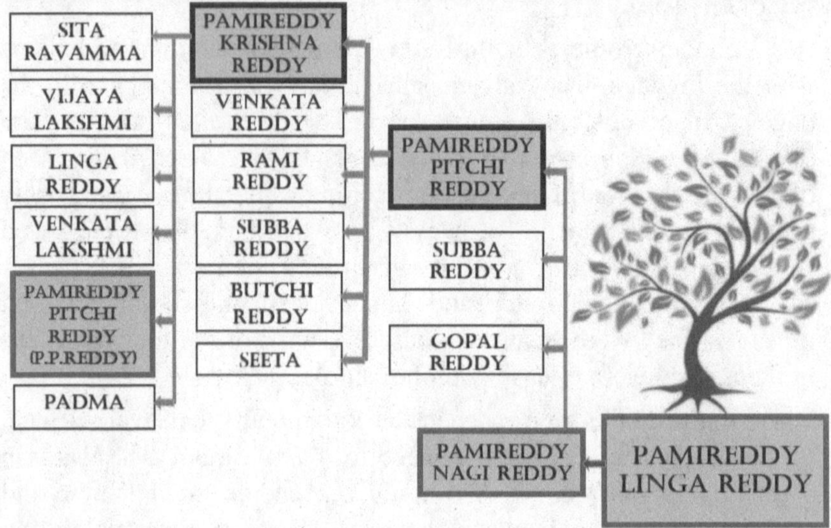

Among Krishna Reddy's children, three were born in Dokiparru and the next three at Jamulapalli.

References

53. (i) Ayyadevara Kaleswarao, "Naa Jeevita Katha-Navya Andhramu."
    Page 413
    (ii) Sri Tummala Venkata Ramaiah. "Bharata Sangrama Charitra"
    Page: 34
54. (i) The details from the interview with Sri Kanumuri Bala Gangadhar
    Tilak: Descendant of Sri Kanamuri Ramireddy
    (ii) Sri Tummala Venkata Ramaiah. Bharata Samgrama Charitra Page:
    111
55. Sri Tummala Venkata Ramaiah. "Bharata Sangrama Charitra" Page: 30
56. Bapu Ramaniyam Atma Katha "Koti Komachi", Page: 30
57. (i) Dr. Lakshmi, V. Vijaya Ph.D., Nagarjuna University Theoretical
    Text, Freedom
    Movement in Krishna District 1905 -1947, Page: 147
    (ii)Interview with Sri Nimmagadda Bhanu Prasad: Descendant of Sri
    Nimmagadda Venkata Krishna Rao

58. (i) Dr. Lakshmi, V. Vijaya Ph.D., Nagarjuna University Theoretical Text, Freedom Movement in Krishna District 1905 -1947, Page: 211,132,147
(ii) Sri Paruchuri Koteshwara Rao, *Telugu Naata Swatantra Sangrama Charitra* Page: 109
(iii) Interview with Sri Pamireddy Venkata Subbarao Reddy: Descendant of Sri Venkata Subbarao Reddy
(iv) Hindu paper Article, 08th September 1936

59. Government bans on Bangore - Malapalli novel - Page. 65 – 67

60. Acharya N.G. Ranga, Economic Organization, pages 20-5, Vol I, Vol II 95 – 100

61. BR Ambedkar speaks on M.K. Gandhi (BBC Radio) https://www.youtube.com/watch?v=_FNSQcEx02A

62. L. Chester.1947 Partition: Drawing of Indo-Pakistani Boundary. Pages: 481-94

63. Tapi Dharmarao, Rallu-Rappalu, Visalandhra Publishing House, Vijayawada 1979, Page-7)

64. E. Subrahmanyam, Gandhiji Ashram Narrative, Daridranarayana Episode. March 1952

65. (i) Dr. Badam Sriramulu, "Biography of Amarajivi Potti Sriramulu," Nagarjuna University Theoretical Book, Page: 52
(ii) Interview with Sri Pamireddy Narayana Reddy: Descendant of Sri Pammareddy Ghantareddy

66. *Abburi Samsmarana Page:199*

67. Interview with Sri Kanumuri Ramireddy: Descendant of Sri Kanumuri Krishnareddy.

68. Thenneti Vishwanadham, Tanguturi Prakasham, "*Naa Jeevitha* Yaatra-4", Page: 640

69. Interview with Sri Lella Kalidas Venkata Ranga Rao(I.P.S): Descendant of Sri Lella Sarabandi.

70. (i) Sri Tummala Venkata Ramaiah. Bharata Samgrama Charitra Page: 121.
(ii) Interview with Sri Kaja Veera Basava Sankarayaya garu: Descendant of Sri Vidiyala Kalahasti Lingam.

71. Ayyadevara Kaleswarao, "Naa Jeevita Katha-Navyaandhramu" Page 343

72. (i) Sri Tummala Venkata Ramaiah. Bharata Samgrama Charitra Page: 121.
(ii) Interview with Sri Ennam Ramakrishna Reddy: Descendant of Sri Gonnuru Sarreddy

73. Thenneti Vishwanadham, Tanguturi Prakasham, "*Naa Jeevitha* Yaatra-4", Page:660

74. Thenneti Vishwanadham, Tanguturi Prakasham, "*Naa Jeevitha* Yaatra-4", Page: 616

75. Janamaddi Hanumashastri Local Governance Magazine, Volume: 10 Shonti Ramamurthy Article, 2011

76. Thenneti Vishwanadham, Tanguturi Prakasham, "*Naa Jeevitha* Yaatra-4", Page: 658

77. Thenneti Vishwanadham, Tanguturi Prakasham, "*Naa Jeevitha* Yaatra-4", Page: 683

78. Thenneti Vishwanadham, Tanguturi Prakasham, "*Naa Jeevitha* Yaatra-4", Page: 694

79. Sri Badam Sriramulu, Ph.D., Amarajivi Potti Sriramulu Biography, Siddhanta Grantham, Nagarjuna University, Page: 221

80. Sri Mandali Buddhaprasad "Krishna Delta Charita Vihanga Veekshanam", page:4

WALKING IN FATHER'S FOOTSTEPS

The native and pure environment of a village creates serene minds. Pamireddy Krishna Reddy used to live in a big, spacious home in Jamulapalli. The house was a space filled with the happiness and pleasure of shared relations. The blossoming of such relations makes place heaven on earth. The entire village folk used to share their work, pain, and happiness without any reservations. After a day's long work in the field, they would assemble at the Rama Temple, share news, pleasantries, and plan the next day's activity. Families would always have dinner together at home. The playful noise and laughter of the kids would fuse energy and life in the village.

Krishna Reddy was always clear-sighted in everything and would employ proper discretion, honesty in all his affairs. He would expect similar honourable conduct in life from all around him. He would always hope the best for others, imagining progress in their lives at every step. He would dream about a progressive society that excelled in every aspect. He used to say that wealth and property are not enough for a society to flourish. The moral strength and wellbeing of all persons in society are also essential. He would not only dream about such a society but constantly work towards building one himself.

Culture – Atla Taddi

Our villages have a strong sense of cultural unity in which almost every festival plays a distinct role. "Atla Taddi" is also one such festival that brings families and all villagers together. Atla Taddi is a festival that honours the married women of every household with presents. The whole family participates in giving away these presents with a clear, established routine, and the event is conducted in a joyful fervour.

The young boys of the village prepare unique artefacts called "Poola Potlam – Flower Packet", literally, on this day. Also called "Uppu Potlam," these are made with dry palm tree seeds and salt-packed in a piece of cloth and packed again in a fresh palm leaf tied tightly. In the evening, all the young men gather in the village centre – between two Rama temples in Jamulapalli's case, and offer these "Poola Potlam" to fire, dancing around. All the kids of the village also gather and take part in the fun.

Jamulapalli's village deity is Maremma. Every year, a procession and celebration would honour the village deity, a major festival for the entire village.

Jolly Childhood

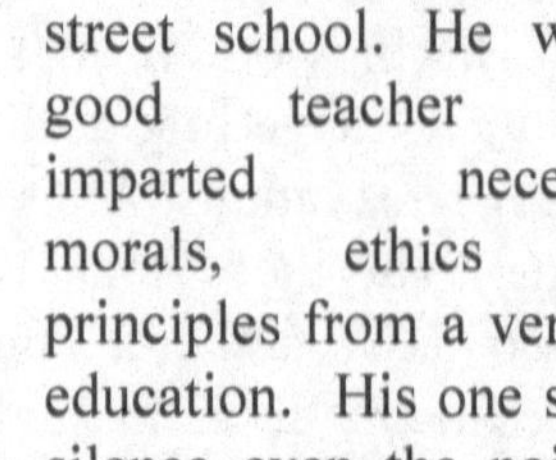

Nagaraju master ran the local village street school. He was a good teacher who imparted necessary morals, ethics and principles from a very early age along with basic education. His one serious glance was enough to silence even the noisiest kids. Peacock feathers were placed inside books by many kids,

with the belief that they would grow and bring good fortune. Kids would run carefree in fields and farmlands, never stopping for bushes or thorns. Unless a thorn was big enough to cause so much pain as to impede walking, kids never bothered about them. But as they had to sit down to study, all kinds of aches and problems would rush back to them. It is as if there is something in the books that would bring out all of the issues in them!

Just around the sunset, flaming torches would be lit up in the house fronts. Kids would sit near them and study, while elders and women also carry out necessary household work there. Pamireddy Linga Reddy shared his memories with his father Krishna Reddy like this:

"Walking to the farm holding my father's hand was a routine we all loved. We used to share so many things with him during those walks. He would tell us to handle small chores in the field with all others. Bringing haystacks for the consumption of cattle was a regular duty. These small activities were ways to make children used to regular farm work. When it was time to gather the farm yield, the kids were made to guess the number of bags the grains would make looking at the dump of yield. He would lift the kid whose estimate was close to the final tally and would give an appreciative kiss. It became a regular competition between the kids. Younger brother P.P Reddy usually won this competition. When we followed his instructions fully, he would hug us and brush our heads lovingly. He would always encourage us to handle our responsibilities and keep up our promises, assuring us that he would always be there to support us.

There used to be a licensing system for bicycles and radios in the sixties. Every year, the licenses had to be renewed by paying the required fee. We used to accompany father to the Pithapuram Municipal office for the cycle license renewal, stand in the queue holding necessary papers. If that work finished early enough, the father would take us to any movie nearby. "Ramudu–Bheemudu" was one movie I remember we saw that way. Later, this licensing system was removed by the government as the number of users grew high.Kids who received lots of love would grow to be persons who would spread love similarly around them as grownups.

We would all go to Dokiparru for Sankranthi. It was a big festival we would celebrate with all our uncles and other close relatives. As if distance increased love among us, our uncles would dote upon us during our stay. Father also used to love all his relatives dearly. He would make every effort to show that he was there for them whenever needed."

✳✳✳

<u>Our Foresight Helped Us</u>

India's main occupation is agriculture. About 90% of the population is dependent on agriculture. Many industries are also agriculture-based. Directly, indirectly agriculture supports crores of the public. The irrigation facilities that were improved in the early days of independence were able to irrigate one crore sixty lakh acres across the country. The gross national income increased by 18%, per capita income by 11%, consumption of goods per head improved by 9%. The abolition of Zamindaris, reformations in the tenant farmers act have created a new environment in the country. Bhakra Nangal, Hirakud Project and other north Indian projects were planned to look at the rising needs. After the successful completion of the first Five-Year Plan, the second and third Five-Year plans were mostly focused on improving the water supply projects in the country. The Nagarjuna Sagar Project was included in the second Five-Year plan after many interesting twists and turns. Finally, on 10th December 1955, Prime Minister Jawahar Lal Nehru laid the foundation stone for the Nagarjuna Sagar Project.

Mukthyala Raja Vasireddy

Nagarjuna Sagar Project was planned as a multipurpose project. The reason behind the evergreen Krishna Delta of the present day; the first dreamer of the Nagarjuna Sagar project was Mukthyala Zamindar "Vasireddy Rama Gopala Krishna Maheshwara Prasad." His dream was his persistence to see the Krishna water spread far and wide in the Andhra region. He constituted a team of retired engineers who worked towards creating an environment favouring the project at the central level.

Sri Vasireddy Rama Gopala Krishna Maheshwara Prasad

Renowned engineer K.L.Rao joined with him, and they together became a force hard to ignore. They met all influential groups to canvas the necessity of the Nagarjuna Sagar Project. They also convened public meetings to raise awareness, established "The Krishna Farmers Welfare Society" to influence the central government through the Madras State government. The Khosla Committee that was constituted to conduct a survey tried to evade visiting the proposed site stating a flimsy reason for no proper roadway. Mukthyala Zamindar intervened and gathered the farmers from 25 villages from the welfare society. After working four days round the clock, a road was laid for the convenience of the committee.

Opposing the transport of Krishna water to Madras, a public meeting was convened by Acharya Ranga at Jaggayyapet. Due to such vocal demands, and the subsequent lobbying by Muktyala Raja and others, the Khosla Committee finalized the project site at Nandi Konda. Muktyala Raja immediately donated 55 thousand acres of land and 52 lakhs of rupees, earning huge praise from Jawahar Lal Nehru. K.L Rao's "Memories of an Engineer" details the events leading to the project.

By 1966, the project was completed and dedicated to the nation by the then Prime Minister Indira Gandhi [81]. Canals were built on both sides of the project to give water to Guntur and Prakasham districts through the right canal, named Jawahar canal; and Nalgonda, Khammam, Krishna and West Godavari districts through the left canal, named Lal Bahadur Shastri canal. The entire length of the Nagarjuna Sagar Dam is 15,080 feet, with 3,900 of it stone made and 11,180 of it gravel made (7,960 feet on the left side, 3,220 feet on the right side).

Architect of the Projects – K.L Rao

It is a river named Krishna. Like any other river, this one also never differentiated between people or areas. It found great satisfaction in flowing through farmer's fields and becoming the food grains that reached their plates. Though it would merge into the sea finally, touching so many lives on its way delighted it.

Careful utilization of this life force would feed generations after generations and create wealth and happiness forever. Intelligent planning and vision for the greater public good are needed to put this never-ending resource to good use and turn any area into a heaven on earth. It would also supply electricity that would change the quality of life throughout.

Engineer Kanoori Lakshmana Rao understood Krishna River's goodness and excellent strength. He took it upon himself to use this boon for the welfare of the entire Andhra region. This determination and commitment to his task made him an unforgettable benefactor to the entire region.

India's first Prime Minister, Jawahar Lal Nehru, described projects as the modern-day temples in our society. Considering this, we could describe K.L Rao as the architect of these temples. During the first Five-Year Plan, K.L Rao designed Nagarjuna Sagar, Kosi, Hirakud, Bhakra Nangal, Farakka, Shree Shailam and Tunga Bhadra projects. His vision and planning led to the secured livelihood and increased food grain production that supported the entire nation.

K.L Rao was born on 15th July 1902, at Kankipadu near Vijayawada in the Krishna district. His father was a lawyer. Rao lost his father at a young age. In a school accident, he lost an eye also. But he never felt deficient and was always a very confident person.

Rao finished his engineering from the Madras University and went on to work as an assistant professor in Burma's Rangoon. In 1939, he secured his PhD from Birmingham University in the UK. He later published a book titled "Structural Engineering: Reinforced Concrete Science." After he came back, he worked in the Madras government as a design engineer. He designed the Rama Pada Sagar Project after Shonthi Venkata Rama Murthy gave him the responsibility during this stint. During the project's building, he insisted that part of the structure be gravel-based to employ the Macharla region where it was built. He considered it his human responsibility to think about the welfare of those displaced locals though there was enough scope to build it entirely stone based.

From 1962 to 1977, he was elected to the Lok Sabha from the Vijayawada constituency as a Congress member. He was the central irrigation and electricity minister in the Nehru, Shastri and Indira cabinets for ten years. Using his excellent understanding of the water resources in India, he wrote a book called "Indian Water Wealth." He was later awarded the "Padma Bhushan".

Between 1966 – 69, annual plans were implemented in the usual Five-Year Plans due to wars with Pakistan and China. Due to the immediate need, the budget allocation mainly was shifted to the military. The irrigation budgets were handed over to respective state governments. This may have led to the water wars between linguistically divided states.

Full Name	Nagarjuna Sagar
Inauguration	1955
Water assignment	281 TMC net water
Barrage capacity	408 TMC
Strategy	21.43 Acres
The length of the main canal	Right canal 203 k.m. Left canal 179 k.m.
Estimated cost	120.67 Crores

<u>Spring to the Rivers</u>

Peddinti Subbi Reddy, son of Pulla Reddy, was born in December 1942 in Jamulapalli village. During his early education (6th and 7th standard), he stayed at Pamireddy Krishna Reddy's residence at Dokiparru to study under Master Varjala Venkatachalam. He studied further at Pithapuram, Anakapalli and Vishakhapatnam to finish his

Engineering degree and went on to work in the Irrigation department for 35 long years, 1965 to 2000. He finally retired as an executive engineer.

Sri Peddinti Subbireddy

He handled project design works, Krishna – Godavari river canals maintenance and oversaw the Polavaram project designs during his tenure. Even after his retirement, he continued to help the department as an expert advisor till 2010. He was an inspiration to many Pakanati youngsters to enter irrigation and water resources management jobs. He named his daughter Krishnaveni as a gesture of respect and love for Pamireddy Krishna Reddy.

***

Anchor Cutoff

When Krishna Reddy came to Dokiparru in 1966, Sankranthi, his younger brothers Rami Reddy and Butchi Reddy implored to shift back to Dokiparru again. Venkata Reddy and Subba Reddy did their biddings with their sister-in-law about the same issue. Somehow, Krishna Reddy decided to accept his brother's request this time. After the year's farming activity and school days were over, the family left Jamulapalli and shifted back to Dokiparru.

Even before all the brothers could celebrate their coming back together, destiny threw a shock at them that would create a vacuum hard to be filled. An elder brother, Krishna Reddy's health, deteriorated mysteriously, and he succumbed to life's finality. Death is an inevitable destination all humans are travelling to, whether slowly or in a hurry. But how one conducts the journey and how many memories they impart to fellow passengers make the ultimate difference.

Krishna Reddy's son P.P Reddy was the hardest hit with his father's sudden demise. The young lad never doubted that his father would be forever with him, just like the Krishna, Godavari Rivers and the Himalayas. He felt as if the entire sky and the stars fell on him, and the earth was swallowing him. His whole energy, life force sapped from him; he felt as if time had stopped and made him a prisoner in this unknown world where he is unable to see his lighthouse.

His father was the strength his entire family gathered around during any small or big hardship. He would carry the kids himself to the doctor when they faced any health issue and sit beside them until they are cured. He would stand as a pillar of support for any person in the village when they lose their family members. He would personally take care of all arrangements and ensure proper rituals are followed at every step. P.P Reddy was recalling the happiness his father felt watching him in new clothes during Deepavali.

But once life is gone, a person is just like a strand of grass that has been cut off. Uncle Rami Reddy was bathing the lifeless body of Krishna Reddy. P.P Reddy went near his brother Linga Reddy, whose eyes were also flooding, and stood with him holding his hand.

Krishna Reddy's wife Bhadramma looked around and saw the sorrow, helplessness the entire family was feeling. She told herself not to cry over spilled milk. She sprung to action, gathering all her inner strength, decided to hold, protect and do everything in her capacity to bring the family back on its feet. She fought against all the problems that threatened the family. She saw how people, society would change when circumstances are not in their favour. She suffered all the hardships herself but never compromised with the future of her children. Though Krishna Reddy's brothers still stood beside her, it was all her strength and grit that kept her family together.

Sri Pamireddy Krishnareddy Shrimati Pamireddy Bhadramma

Thorny Life

Bhadramma came from a small village that never saw any huge hardships. After her marriage, she saw how women in joint families of Krishna, Guntur districts fight over silly things. After becoming a big family member, she saw how family members differentiate between people with different incomes, abilities, and properties. She felt that the human values passed down from many generations had been trashed by these Krishna – Guntur district younger generations. Jealousy, laziness, ineptitude, cheating, guile, selfishness, avarice and all other bad emotions have taken over and are ruling these people.

Sometimes, it is difficult for people to lose their bad habits, despite either good advice or some innate sense even they might still have. Even some great persons are seen losing their high position caught up in these evil influences. Bhadramma's lone fight for her family should have evoked sympathy and genuine support from all around, but it was not so. The strangeness of society creates more impediments in somebody's path, especially when they are alone and fighting. Society would criticize, make fun of, heckle and point fingers at the efforts and methods of these warriors. They might be dubbed wrong, adamant or even more by this society.

The Indian Hindu society strongly believes in rebirth though there are hardly any definitive proofs for it. Something in this direction happened after Krishna Reddy's passing away too. Precisely on the 13th day of his death, as if he had decided to come back to handle unfinished stuff in his life, Krishna Reddy's second daughter Vijaya Lakshmi gave birth to a son. Bhadramma felt that her husband has come back in this form and named the newborn Venkata Krishna Reddy. This child alleviated a lot of pain Bhadramma felt after losing her husband.

At a later stage, Bhadramma tried to borrow some money from a village elder. This man could have simply rejected her request; instead,

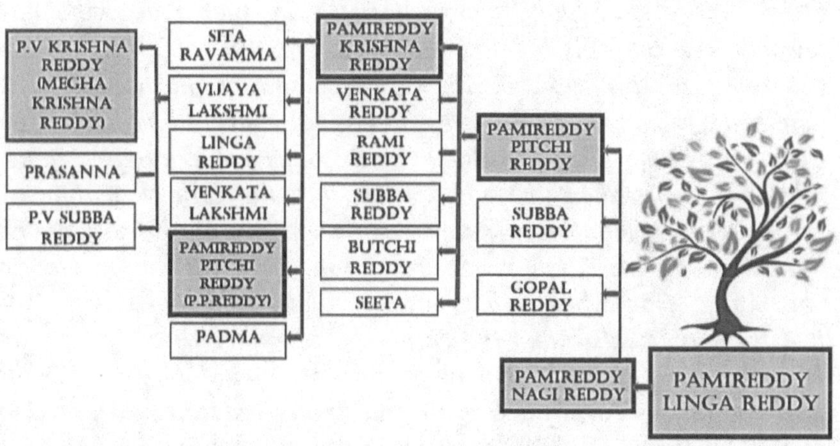

he made her visit him again and again, every time telling her to come again to take the money. Poor Bhadramma humiliated herself due to the heartlessness of this person. Such un helping, egotistic persons would end up "mad", "murderous" and themselves would not be helped when they need it. This is the direct result of their sadistic, selfish behaviour.

When people who suffered a lot in life decide to help those in need, they would be forced to face unnecessary difficulties for their good intentions. People who are born into good fortune hardly ever care for others in need. Few of them even feel that their fortunes are dependent on others staying poor and sad. Others usually decide a person's character by watching how he behaves with others.

Every man desires love, wealth and fame. Love is needed in young age, fame in old age, but wealth is required all the time. Wealth could bring both love and fame whenever required.

Bhadramma was making a trip to her parent's house to attend a marriage with son P.P Reddy accompanying her. P.P Reddy took a coin from his mother. A vision struck him as he held it, showing the journey that coin might have had until then.

The Copper Anna's Journey

"A big block of copper was melted first and poured onto a plate of small blocks in the size of an anna coin. At the Mint, these blocks were printed with letters and numbers we generally find on all coins. These coins were then sent to a bank. This bank gave these coins to a businessman during a transaction. He was such a miser that any money that went into his big safe would never see the light again. He died holding all his money. All the sons shared the wealth. The particular anna coin went to a son who had all kinds of bad habits and reached a prostitute. That prostitute bought some grocery that evening, and the coin reached an oil seller. After this, the coin went into the pockets of several rich men, where it was rested for a few days each and sent away again. One day, it reached a rickshaw pullers hand. He put it into his pocket, from where it fell onto the road as the pocket had holes in it. A few street kids found the coin, who promptly gave it to a fruit seller and enjoyed the fruits sharing among them. It did not stay with the fruit seller much, went around a bit and finally reached Dokiparru to tell this entire story to P.P Reddy during that train journey."

The train was on the Kovvuru, Rajamandry Bridge; by this time, P.P Reddy threw the coin into river Godavari and asked the river to bless him. The coin slowly reached the cold bed of the river and settled into the soft sand and plankton at the bottom, where it was not to be disturbed for a long, long time.

Bhadramma drew her son closer and told him that *"It is good to respect the forces of nature around you. But throwing money is not the right way to do it, as it would mean that you are not giving the proper respect to money by doing this. Use the money wisely. Think about using, controlling the forces of nature with your intellect and the proper utilization of money. This way you will become a special person, one in a million. Think about these terms. Don't just follow others blindly, like you just did with that coin."* Just then, another mother was telling her kid about how water naturally flows to the downside.

P.P Reddy was trying to understand and digest all this information and knowledge.

What is water?

How can water go upwards?

How do trees on a hill sustain?

What if the percentage of water in a human body falls below 70%?

Why is about 96.5% of the water on the earth not drinkable

As P.P Reddy was wrestling with these questions in his head, the train had reached Pithapuram, and they sat on a bullock cart that would carry them to Jamulapalli village.

China's Attack

The political environment deep within the villages of the country started deteriorating rapidly. More and more parties were becoming greedy for power and started fomenting division, rivalry, class, caste consciousness in the general public. It was all for the sake of power and profit through power. Ethics and values were not just taking a back seat but were being entirely jettisoned for few seats and a shot at power. Public representatives were more answerable, subservient to the party than the public and constitution itself.

The growing class consciousness was creating new kinds of rifts in public. The two main ways were both leading to the same kind of evil. One was adopting violent methods to grab power; the other was using violent means to hold on to power once it has secured it. One was leading to a dictatorship that could not be tolerated; the other was turning into crushing imperialism.

Humanity would suffer deeply under any of these systems. The freedom and safety of humanity were at stake. One was like a disease without a cure; the other was a bottomless ocean.

Communism looks good on paper and in general talk. But even communist countries also stigmatize, hunt and kill those people who question their methods.

Under these circumstances, China attacked India. It was a deep shock to the trust we had in our neighbour. ***"Whatever bad forces try at any level, but India, China, Soviet friendship is so deep that it is unbreakable,"*** wrote poet Sri-Sri in his "Moscow Yatra." Suddenly the bond was breached. Trusting a communist country blindly was a big mistake on India's part. Indian communists were shell shocked and had nothing to say. All the books that sung about China and Russia turned scrap used as packing material in shops. The entire country lost their faith in communism. The party cadres also fought among themselves and broke into three splinter groups.

People with foresight had long been warning that trusting China could be dangerous. When this turned into reality, Nehru could not show his face to the public. The country had to run for America's help.

Prime Minister's Signature – Stains of Blood

Lal Bahadur Shastri had invigorated and united the entire country with his slogan – "Jai Jawan – Jai Kisan". Despite being a

Sri Lal Bahadur Shastri

leader of long-standing, he was known for his simplicity and honesty. When Nehru passed away suddenly in 1964, Shastri took up the responsibilities and became the second prime minister. In 1965, the issues between India and Pakistan escalated to newer levels, and Pakistan suddenly attacked India.

Shastri was known for his toughness also, and he rose to the occasion to give a befitting reply to the neighbour on all fronts. A 17-day long war took place, and the resurgent Indian leadership under Shastri was hard to handle for the enemy. The entire country rallied behind Shastri and was ready for any sacrifice to protect the country's sovereignty. The United Nations, America and Russia came in between, and long discussions took place to re-establish peace between the neighbours.

Tashkent, which is now in Uzbekistan, was the place where these peace talks were held. On 10th January 1966, Prime Ministers of both Pakistan and India – Ayub Khan and Shastri, signed on a peace deal brokered by the facilitators. The Tashkent Peace Accord was more in favour of Pakistan, the first perpetrator. Despite winning in the war, India was forced to sign this deal that did not serve its interests. India lost the power to attack Pakistan for the proxy war it had been raging in Kashmir for a long. The very next day, after signing the deal, PM Shastri died in Tashkent in mysterious circumstances.

PM's wife, Lalitha Shastri, expressed serious doubts over the circumstances of his death, alleging a poison attack [82]. Several parties expressed the same doubts, but a post-mortem was not conducted to verify these doubts. A butler who served Shastri was rumoured to have laced his food with poison. India officially declared that the PM died of a heart attack. Because India did not press much, even Russia hogwash the incident and declared that the butler was innocent. The Congress party also stayed mum largely. It was rumoured that America's CIA also might have played a role in this death.

The Indian Prime Minister's office released a statement that releasing any information about this incident would spoil foreign relations of the country and ceased all information under the official secrets act.

When Janatha Party came into power, a committee was appointed under the headship of Raj Narayan. Shastri's personal doctor and assistant, who were going to give a statement before this committee, met with an accident. The persons who caused the accident left them seriously injured. The doctor succumbed to the injuries, and the assistant lost his memory, deepening the mystery surrounding Shastri's death.

Operation Focus

Peddinti Butchi Reddy, son of Raja Reddy, was born in Jamulapalli on 4th September 1937. His early education took place under Varjala Venkatachalam Master and later at Gudlavalleru High School. After his graduation, he studied aeronautical engineering from the Aeronautical Society of India and took an associate membership. The duty there took him from Kalaikundi Air Force Station to the country's major air force stations. He participated in active duty in Indo-Pak War, assisted in the Bangladesh Liberation War. In 1965, at

WALKING IN FATHER'S FOOTSTEPS

Adampur Air Force Station, Jalandhar few Pakistani warplanes flew under the radar and bombed the runway. The attack damaged few planes parked in the hangar and spoiled the runway to some extent. Butchi Reddy narrowly escaped death in the attack. The next day, PM Lal Bahadur Shastri visited Adampur Station in solidarity and, among many others, spoke with Butchi Reddy also to know the events of the attack.

Butchi Reddy recalled that the PM later conducted a meeting on that very same damaged runway and addressed the Air Force personnel, giving them confidence and a renewed spirit of patriotism. "If even one such act is repeated, there won't be a Pakistan," thundered PM Shastri, recounted Butchi Reddy [83].

In December 1971, when the Indian Air Force was taking part in Operation Focus along with the Israeli Air Force, Butchi Reddy was working at the Silchar Airbase in Assam. This Airbase played an instrumental role in the Bangladesh Liberation War in crushing the Pakistani forces. The Prime Minister, Indira Gandhi, visited the Base and infused the soldiers with confidence. Butchi Reddy handled the key Helicopter Landing Officer duties at that time. He later worked as the in-

Sri Peddinti Bucchireddy with his wife, Seetaravamma

charge of Cochin Airlines Station.

Mulki Rules

The anti-Hindi movement in 1968 brought all college students of Sarkar Districts onto the roads. The academic year was entirely lost. The student leaders finally submitted to the then Chief Minister Kasu Brahmananda Reddy to not force the Hindi language on them and rested the movement. The tri language system in education was introduced as a result of this.

The Urdu word "Mulki" means "Native." In 1915, Hyderabad's ruler Nizam introduced Mulki Rules to ensure reservation of local posts to the natives [84]. Later, in 1956, The Gentlemen's Agreement reintroduced this rule. But because this rule was largely neglected and deemed inoperable, the Telangana people have always been dissatisfied in the united Andhra Pradesh.

Politics within the State went on changing with the times. Jalagam Vengala Rao (Velama) did not find a place in Kasu Brahmananda Reddy's ministry, which led him to start a separate Telangana agitation in Khammam. This movement spread to other parts of Telangana, leading to great unrest. The Mulki Rules came to the forefront again. There were rumours that by 28th February 1969, the Andhra nativity employees in Telangana will be sent back to the Andhra region. Central Government was believed to be considering sending the Auditor General to see the allocation of surplus funds between the regions. The Separate Telangana Movement had gained prominence, and the fervour had reached a feverish pitch.

Marri Chenna Reddy, Konda Lakshman Bapuji unveiled a new party Telangana Praja Samithi, at Osmania University, with the students giving it full support. The entire Telangana was bursting with dharnas, hartals, rasta rokos, train blockades etc. The law & order was on the brink of collapse. Police were resorting to lathi-charge and firing routinely. Along with political activists, school- teachers also sat on relay hunger strikes across the region. It was chaos all around. Schools, colleges, offices were closed.

As a response to the separate Telangana Movement, "The Jai Andhra Movement" came up in 1972 in the Seemandhra region. The students of the Seemandhra region feared that the implementation of Mulki rules would reduce their chances in job recruitments and supported the Jai Andhra Movement [85]. In response to these volatile conditions, Indira Gandhi's government announced the "Six Point Formula" in 1973. Keeping up with her reputation as a tough lady, Indira ruled out the formation of Telangana outright. The region's backwardness was to be addressed with better governance and special schemes paving the way for the region's development. Forming a separate state for such reason would lead to many more such demands, felt Indira. Thus, the separate Telangana Movement was crushed brutally by 1973.

Journey Back to the Place of Birth

Sri Vellanki Purnachander Rao

Vellanki Purnachander Rao, son of Kutumba Rao was born in 1943 in Dokiparru. In 1968, when he was working as a school- teacher in Medak government school, during the agitation demanding implementation of Mulki Rules and separate Telangana, he resigned from his job and returned to Dokiparru. He established a school after coming back and rededicated himself to the cause of educating the youth of the region and relentlessly worked towards giving them a better future.

Many of his students have served the nation as IAS, IPS, lawyers, and many other important positions. Purnachander Rao's outstanding contribution has become a lasting service to the country in the form of his students.

References

81. Jawahar Lal Nehru, "The Making of India," 1989
82. *Lalita Ke Aansoo,* written by Krant M. L. Verma, 1978
83. Interview with Peddinti Butchi Reddy
84. Article by Digavalli Venkata Sivarao. Andhra Prabha 02-12-1972
85. Ravinutala Sriramulu, "Mahitatmudu Sri Mandali Venkata Krishna Rao" Book. Page: 30

MIRAGES OF THE DESERT

Across the country, disputes have been raging over the sharing of river water frequently. Upper riparian states are also insisting on the reallocation of waters based on rising requirements. It is these same states that preferred political agreements over expert advice in this matter. The Bachavat Tribunal award came in 1973, around the time when the agitations for separate states were just dying down in Telugu regions. The Bachavat award benefited the Andhra region, but the Rayalaseema region lost its right over the Krishna water entirely.

As the doctrine of prior appropriation tells, water allocations to already running projects were confirmed first. Because there were enough projects already constructed in the Andhra region, there was no problem in this area. Maharashtra and Karnataka did not construct many projects by then, so, naturally, they felt bad about assured allocation to older projects. Bachavat tribunal reduced the calculations of water availability in Krishna River from 2060 T.M.C to 1693.36 T.M.C and allocated these waters to three states, exempting Tamil Nadu.

Under this new allocation, Andhra share came down from earlier 56.3% (1165 T.M.C) to 44.5% (754 T.M.C). Karnataka was given 600 T.M.C and Maharashtra 400 T.M.C Later, Hafiz Muhammad Ibrahim redistributed the water again, as per which Andhra share was reduced again from 44.5% to 38.9%. Accordingly, Karnataka share rose from 33.3% to 33.7% and Maharashtra share from 22.2% to 27.4%. Overall, from 1951, the Andhra share of Krishna water had gone down by 17.4%.

Regarding Godavari River water allocations, the central government attitude gave scope to more and more controversies and fights between the riparian states. Allocation of Godavari water has been in discussions for six years before the Bachavat Committee. After almost fifteen years, under the guidance of the central irrigation ministry; Andhra, Maharashtra, Karnataka, Madhya Pradesh and Orissa have come to an understanding and started paying close attention to addressing their water needs.

For many decades, thousands of T.M.C of water is flooding into the sea through Krishna and Godavari rivers, but the Telugu political leadership never took it seriously. All the present-day disputes over river water allocations are caused by the selfishness of politicians in the area only, but not by the people here.

Union with the Sea

A canal called "Ramula Kaluva," a subsidiary of "Pulleru Canal" dug by Arthur Cotton, begins at Pamarru and stops at MamidiKolla village. Dokiparru farmers thus became outskirt farmers of this Ramula Canal. The dependence on this canal never really favoured Dokiparru farmers. Though it was flowing at a touching distance, the water was always too far for Dokiparru farmers. To alleviate this problem, Kanuri Damodarayya (Kavutaram), Kanumuri Krishna Reddy (Dokiparru), and BuragaddaNiranjan Rao (Kankata) dug a new gravity canal from Pulleru near Gudlavalleru to Kankata via Dokiparru with their personal funds. They called it "Singarayi Canal." When this canal route was found to be going over the Dokiparru Nagendra Swami temple, the issue was solved after discussions and the canal route was adjusted not to touch the temple.

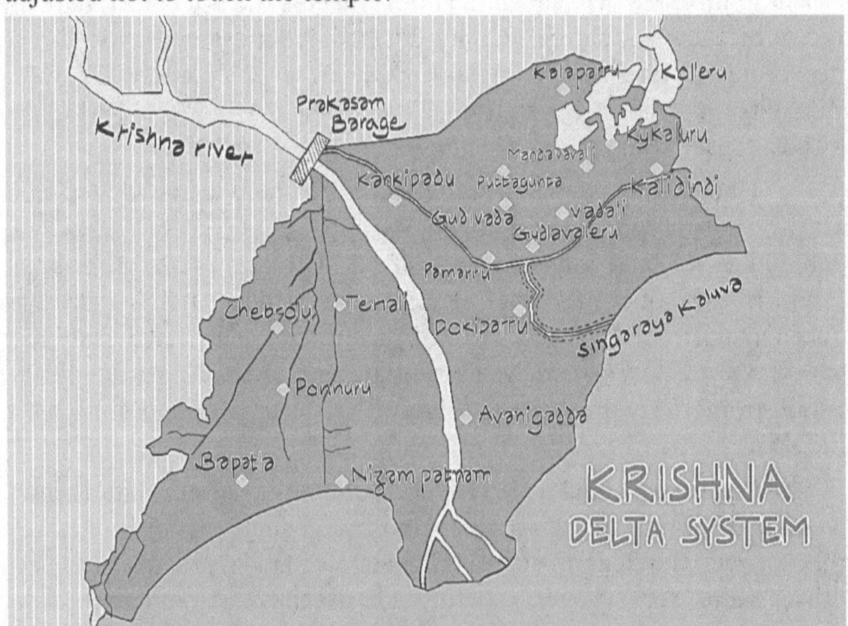

The drinking water deficiency of the Dokiparru people was solved with this canal. Sometimes it may not serve well to depend too much on the government; at the same time, any development activity has to take enough care not to hurt any local sentiments even if it is serving public interests only.

Farmer – Water

"The Cracks in the Soil… In this Land of Famine… In a Long Wait for a Dark Cloud…" It was as if Mother India is standing in front of the House of Legislation with a begging bowl and crying for some water and food. But these governments do not show interest in farmers' issues as much as they show in collecting levy's, drainage cess and other such taxes. Due to no support from the government and dependence on nature, private investors and such, the simple thinking farmers are getting into a chain of interests, bad loans and failing crops. These farmers do not need a religion, god, or caste politics… all they need is water, even if it is limited, they will manage.

Indira Gandhi government in the centre in 1976 removed the D.M.K government from the rule in Tamilnadu and brought the State under President's rule. In 1977, when Indira came to Tamilnadu for the election campaign, she made a promise of bringing Krishna water to Madras through a special project –Telugu Ganga. She pushed this decision onto the state governments of her party in Andhra Pradesh, Karnataka and Maharashtra, without listening to their objections or concerns in water sharing.

An agreement was signed for Andhra, Karnataka and Maharashtra to allocate five T.M.C each, with a total of 15 T.M.C to be sent to Madras by this Telugu Ganga project. All the central political leaders considered it their first duty to alleviate the water problems of Madras. Renowned engineer K.L Rao brought out all the behind screens issues and compromises made while reaching this agreement.

DiviSeema Floods

Krishna River divides into two streams to form DiviSeema Island. It is a place known for its fine arts and dance. Kuchipudi, the famous village named after a dance form; Movva village, the birthplace of famous balladeer Kshetrayya, are part of DiviSeema[86]. 19th November 1977 is an unforgettable day in the history of the Krishna district. By that afternoon, a dangerous storm had brewed in the sea that unleashed itself upon Krishna Delta's Avanigadda region. The sea waves measuring over six meters pounded upon the villages in its path.

Howling winds at unimaginable speeds devastated all of the Krishna and Guntur districts.

It looked as if the rain would never stop. The wind speed crossed 200 kilometres per hour[87]. Trees, electric poles, telephone poles pulled out of their bases. Just after two hours of intense rain, thousands of dead bodies were floating everywhere. The heavy loss of life and property led to countrywide fund collection by all to aid rehabilitation efforts.

Sri Manadali Venkata Krishna Rao

Even silver screen idol N.T Rama Rao took to the streets with a begging bowl and collected funds along with newspapers. Political leaders were quick to observe that N.T.R had political motives behind his appearance. Ramakrishna Mission built thousands of homes and donated them to the needy. The government also made plans to construct many storm shelters along the shore.

Mother Theresa visited the place and spent some time in rehabilitation work. Mandali Venkata Krishna Rao worked day and night with complete dedication, coordinating with many voluntary organisations that came for help and restored emergency needs and minimum necessities for the public [88].

First Step to Polavaram

In 1980, due to the dissidence against CM Chenna Reddy, the Congress central leadership removed him from the post and T. Anjayya, who was the Labor Affairs minister in Indira's central cabinet, was installed as the CM of Andhra.

Sri Tanguturi Anjayya

Tanguturi Anjayya, son of Papi Reddy, was born on 16th August 1919 at Bhanur village in Medak district. His life was full of many dramatic twists and turns. He lost both his parents at an early age. Young Anjayya realised that his close relatives were more interested in his property than his welfare and considered it a risk to his life in staying with them. He took the extreme step of leaving his place of birth forever. One night he walked up to the nearby village Shankar Palli railway station and got on a train that was leaving for Hyderabad. He got down at Nampalli Railway Station, walked up to Sulthan Bazar and took refuge in an Orphans Home for some time. His birth name was Tanguturi Rama Krishna Reddy. Fearing harm from his close relatives, he changed his name to Talla Anjayya, borrowing it from the in-charge of the Orphan's Home, whose surname was Talla, who belonged to the Yadava community.

Anjayya finished his education at the Sulthan Bazar High School. He had to work as daily labour at Allwyn Factory at a rate of 6 anna's per day to meet his requirements. As he lived close to working-class S.C.'s and B.C. communities most of his life, he identified himself with the hard-working, daily wage community more. He rose to be a labour leader and got into active politics as a union leader.

He later won as an M.P on the Telangana Praja Samithi ticket. After the party merged with Congress later, he got into the close circuit of Sanjay Gandhi. He was also close to P.V. Narasimha Rao.

Because of his knowledge of Hindi and Urdu, he could do well in Delhi politics. As a member of Sanjay Gandhi's inner circle, his visibility was significant. All these factors helped him in getting the C.M's post. He later won from the Ramayampet assembly constituency.

After becoming the CM as a dissident leader, he inducted all of the dissident leaders into the state ministry, leading to the formation of the biggest state ministry the country has ever seen, with 61 members. It was his ploy to avoid any accusations of not giving a chance to young leaders. He openly spoke about the different recommendations each leader had in the press meet. He thus pushed the blame of the jumbo ministry onto other leaders. Later, he reduced the size of the ministry considerably as the central government was forced to recommend a smaller ministry. Chandrababu Naidu's first post as a minister was in Anjayya's ministry for the Library, Cinematography departments. Y.S Rajashekhara Reddy's first post as a minister was also with Anjayya, as the Rural Development minister. Another young leader that was encouraged by Anjayya was P Janardhana Reddy.

It is believed that during Anjayya's term, N.T RamaRao desired to be appointed member of the Rajyasabha and lobbied for it.

Anjayya brought down the voting age from 21 to 18 in a daring step. He started conducting elections for Panchayati Raj and Municipals and also called for direct election of Sarpanch, Panchayat Presidents. All these daring steps brought him wide appreciation.

After Sanjay Gandhi died in an aeroplane accident, Anjayya's good days declined. Though Nadendla Bhaskara Rao was given an Agriculture portfolio in his ministry, Nadendla openly disregarded

Anjayya's power. He took up the position of number two in the government and would command ministries, M.L.A.s and officers openly. His highhandedness irked Anjayya, and after some time, he dismissed him from the ministry.

When Chenna Reddy found a similar fault with Nadendla in the previous ministry, he shifted him to an archaeology portfolio and left him in that insignificant position. After Anjayya removed Nadendla from the ministry, he sent a 17-page note to PM Indira Gandhi on Anjayya.

Even as the Chief Minister, Anjayya led a very simple life. He was closest to the poor and downtrodden. Even during political meetings, he would instruct to feed the drivers and press people first. Poet Dasharadhi declared that the language spoken by Anjayya is perfect Telugu when people made several jokes on his dialect. But the media continued to portray Anjayya as a ruffian, uncouth, joker like figure.

As the chief minister, he went to receive PM's son Rajiv Gandhi at the airport during a visit. Many party activists and the general public also gathered in great numbers to welcome Rajiv as his clout was on the rise. Anjayya and others were waiting on the runway with garlands and bouquets to make a grand show. Himself a pilot, Rajiv Gandhi admonished Anjayya, somewhat sternly, for carrying flowers etc., so close to the plane as it could lead to an accident if caught in the propellers. He is reported of using the word "Buffoon..." addressing Anjayya. The papers carried it prominently the next day; Anjayya's image was damaged further.

In 1954, Jawaharlal Nehru described irrigation projects as the new temples. But from the Third Five-Year Plan, any proposals of projects from the southern states were replied with the comment "Disease of Gigantism" and rejected.

Later, Captain Dinshaw Dastoor proposed to carry floodwater to famine-stricken areas under a scheme named "Garland of Hope." This way, the water supply capacities will increase, navigation facilities will improve through rivers, leading to many economic and social benefits, he explained. The Janatha Government in 1978 brought forward this "Garland of Hope" into the forefront again[89]. But unfortunately, the government fell within three years without taking any further steps on the scheme.

But Andhra CM Anjayya took inspiration from the scheme and took it upon himself to link Godavari and Krishna rivers to solve all water issues in the State. Going ahead with the plan, he laid the foundation stone for the Polavaram project on 19th May 1981. The irrigation department was ordered to prepare detailed estimates and plans.

Rushing the affairs

Oleti Rami Reddy, son of PapaRao was born on 20th May 1955 in Narasingapuram village of Pakanati region. He was an engineer in the irrigation department. In 1980, he was working in the Kovvuru division, and upon Anjayya's orders, he rushed forward with making plans and estimates for the Polavaram project. An initial estimate for 750 crore rupees was prepared[90]. Rami Reddy later worked in

Sri Oleti Rami Reddy

the Dhavaleshvaram division before finally retiring in the year 2013.

What happened to Telugu Pride?

Politics is a game just like cricket, unpredictable and exciting. Nadendla Bhasker Rao, who was expelled from Congress, joined the newly formed Telugu Desam Party by N.T.R. The rejection of a Rajya Sabha seat pushed N.T.R to take up the "Telugu Pride" slogan and form the Telugu Desam Party.

Sri N.T Rama Rao(N.T.R)

Around the time of establishing the Telugu Desam Party in 1982, N.T.R did everything with an eye for political motive. He carefully chose only films with patriotic, message-oriented stories (Justice Chowdary, Bobbili Puli, NaaDesham…) leading up to the formation of the party.

His main support and guide informing the party, Nadendla Bhasker Rao, had ample political experience and acumen. After Sanjay Gandhi's demise, his wife Maneka Gandhi started a party with the name "Sanjay Vichar Manch." Nadendla Bhasker Rao facilitated an understanding with Maneka Gandhi and N.T.R, and both parties fought the 1983 elections together[91]. The victory in the election was claimed entirely by the Telugu Desam Party. After this first big victory in the political arena, N.T.R's natural arrogance grew exponentially. He felt that it was entirely his charisma that won such widespread acceptance for them. Nadendla claimed that it was his political planning that brought notoriety and identity to the new entrant. Ramoji Rao, on the other side, claimed that it was his wide publicity and positive portrayal in the media that paved the way for the victory.

Six months had passed. After a heavy, noisy discussion in the legislative council, Ramoji Rao's Eenadu gave a headline to the news "Peddala sabhalo galabha – Ruckus in the Elder's Council!". The title resulted in a huge uproar for the use of the word "Galabha – Ruckus." The Council gave notice to Ramoji Rao to personally appear and apologise. When Ramoji Rao did not respond to the notice, the City Police Commissioner was ordered to arrest and bring him to the House. The issue had reached the level of a constitutional crisis. N.T.R advised Ramoji over a call to not aggravate the issue anymore and respect the orders of the Council. Ramoji was completely miffed with N.T.R and the party, as he considered himself the backbone and biggest contributor to the party's victory.

The other media houses did not get into this controversy as it could have led to more complications. They could not support their fellow publisher; neither could they openly call for his surrender and further anger him.

As Congress was planning for a big public meeting on 23rd March 1984 in Gunturu with Indira Gandhi, N.T.R's T.D.P conducted a big meeting along with seven other anti congress parties one week earlier on 18th March 1984. The meeting was a big success. N.T.R got carried away looking at the big crowd and said one or two harsh things about Indira Gandhi. State's Information Minister Chegondi HariRama Jogayya declared that N.T.R has an element of divinity in him, and he is destined to occupy the big seat in Delhi [92].

Ramoji Rao approached the Supreme Court as he was not willing to apologise to the Legislative Council in person. N.T.R had to support Ramoji as the issue kept escalating. On 06th April 1984, the central government issued a statement suggesting that if the issue is not resolved, the central rule might be imposed in the State [93].

The Labor minister in the State raised new allegations of corruption in the government, with a plan to divert the public view from the other controversy. There were number of news circulating with allegations of highhanded decisions by Nadendla Bhasker Rao in the ministry. It was rumoured that the Nadendla faction could vote against the party interests in the upcoming Rajyasabha elections.

As alleged, there was cross-voting in the elections, but not to the tune of rumoured projections. Telugu Desham leadership was in two minds about taking disciplinary action on the few dissident M.L.A.s. Though there were no proofs that Nadendla was behind the dissidence, he was criticised and derided in the Vishakhapatnam Mahanadu meeting. Nallapureddy Srinivasulu Reddy was also humiliated as Nadendla's cohort. T.D.P's chief secretary Upendra tried to discourage such ill-mannered behaviour, but the party cadres acted as if being directed by some from the above.

M.L.A.s who had no connection with the cross-voting were also forced to come before the disciplinary committee and apologise. Mudragada Padmanabham was one such person. Irked Mudragada released a statement saying that untoward incidents were happening in the party. In a subsequent meeting that took place in Yanamala Ramakrishnudu's residence on 18th May 1984, Gorantla Bucchayya Chowdary was exhorted to openly attack and humiliate Mudragada. T.D.P favouring media houses, wrote that Nadendla should not be given command of the party and government when N.T.R would go to America for medical tests.

On 24th July 1984, Indira Gandhi attended a public meeting in Medak. Around that time, the "Telugu Pride slogan" was brought forward again, alleging the centre to have humiliated the C.M by not announcing proper allowances for his treatment in America. In the National Development Council meeting, N.T.R made a big show by staging a walkout along with the C.M.s of five other states, alleging discrimination.

The Congress party lost power in the State for the first time due to T.D.P, and it was unable to digest the humiliation at the hands of a rookie. It was looking for an opportunity to strike back. When Indira attended the Medak meeting, she spent nine hours in the State touring around. In between, she had a half-hour meeting with Nadendla Bhasker Rao at his residence and asked him to come back to Congress. Thus, the stage for Nadendla's revolt in T.D.P was set [94].

August 1984 was an exciting time in the State's political climate. The Machiavellian machinations of Nadendla Bhasker Rao came to full fruition, and N.T.R's government was finally brought down. Nadendla became the new chief minister. Governor Ramlal gave him thirty days to prove his majority in the House. Utilising the available time, N.T.R's coterie did everything it could to disturb the M.L.A.s in Nadendla's camp. N.T.R gathered all his M.L.A.s, took them to Karnataka and held them in a hotel called Das Prakash, with the support of Karnataka C.M Ramakrishna Hegde. This was the first-ever instance that a party resorted to holding up M.L.A.s supporting it in a camp like a setup.

N.T.R's supporters made a lot of noise at the central level, saying that a legally elected first non-congress government was being brought down in an unconstitutional way. A big public meeting was conducted in Vijayawada to gather public support. The public did not care much for this largely political drama. The media network supporting N.T.R relentlessly wrote about the political controversy. It was as if a lie travels half the world around while the truth is still putting on its shoes.

There is a Telugu saying that means "A Karanam's grudge doesn't rest even when the opponent has reached the graveyard." P.V. Narasimha Rao, a well-learned Telugu Karanam, is respected far and wide for his knowledge, but he is also an astute politician. Acharya N.G Ranga, K.L.N. Prasad (Rajya Sabha M.P), Dr. Y Nayudamma approached P.V. Narasimha Rao to discuss the issue of N.T.R's government. P.V told them that N.T.R's request will be considered if he personally visits Indiramma and tenders his apology[95]. The message was conveyed to N.T.R

N.T.R found it hard to accede to this demand. He preferred to reject this offer. But many elders around him convinced that it was just a method of solving a dispute in a friendly meeting. N.T.R had to accept.

After 20 days, when Indira Gandhi came on a visit to Bangalore, N.T.R went to the Raj Bhavan there and met her. There were rumours that M.G.R was also part of the mediation and was present at that meeting. Karnataka CM Hegde criticised that M.G.R surrendered to Congress for the water promised to Madras through Telugu Ganga.

All of Nadendla's efforts came to a nought. His blind trust in Indira Gandhi brought him down again. He confided with his friends that after Chandrababu came into the party, he had been having a tough time.

During a visit of P.V. Narasimha Rao to the State, who was the Central Home Minister then, State Home Minister Chegondi Harirama Jogayya visited him as per protocol. P.V told Chegondi that Congress would like to work along with T.D.P regardless of the reduced clout of the party. "Convey this as my personal message to N.T.R," said P.V. When Chegondi tried to detail his meeting with P.V, N.T.R burst out, saying he doesn't want to hear his name. Chegondi was shocked, with some effort; he managed to convey the message and kept quiet without offering any further opinion[96].

During the elections next year, Chegondi was initially rejected a ticket by N.T.R. But Secretary Upendra implored N.T.R to change his decision based on the support Chegondi has in the caste groups. After winning, N.T.R did not give Chegondi any ministry this time.

N.T.R's anger for P.V continued, and he announced the removal of Munasab and Karanam posts entirely in the village level administration in 1985. Reddy's who held the Munasab posts mostly were not affected much by this decision, but the Niyogi Brahmins (like P.V), who held the Karanam posts, were devastated due to the decision as their main skill set had become useless suddenly. They had to migrate, take up odd jobs to provide for their families. Most of the Niyogi families fell to bad times and lost their identity in society entirely. The larger society also did not react to their problems, as they remembered the hardships these Karanams inflicted upon all.

N.T.R's Telugu Ganga

The Telugu Ganga project was exclusively proposed to tackle the water problems of Madras city. It was brought forward again in 1984 under the Telugu Desam government. As per agreements, the project's entire cost was to be borne by the Tamil Nadu government. Canals would be dug between Shreeshailam to Poondi to supply the fifteen T.M.C water allotted. Andhra had no personal benefit with the Telugu Ganga project at all. Even on the route of the canals, the Rayala Seema farmers of the adjoining areas were prohibited from using the water [97]. In a strange imposition of the rule, if any farmer grew any crop using the water, government officials would come and destroy the entire crop.

This was a strange agreement the Telugu government signed, disregarding the needs of its own public in favour of some far off lands. The Rayalaseema public was the biggest losers as they had lost their rightful water while facing severe drought conditions themselves. As per the 1977 agreements, water should be released to this project only for a period of 3 to 4 months from the Shreeshailam reservoir. When the project was finally implemented in 1984, N.T.R's government changed these rules without any information to Karnataka, which was a partner to the agreement. When Karnataka asked why it was not consulted, N.T.R had no answer.

"Because of my association with Madras, I am sanctioning this project as a gesture of thanks," said N.T.R at the completion of this project. This goodwill project is a direct result of the Bangalore Rajbhavan meeting between N.T.R and Indira, mediated by M.G.R. The "Telugu Pride" is visible only in the media, not in protecting the rights of the Telugu people!

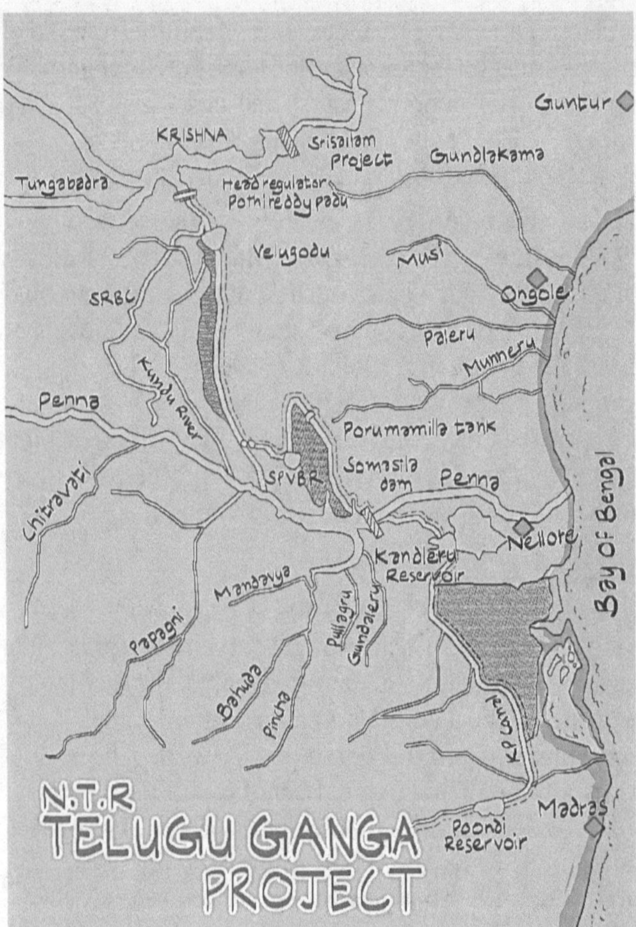

After Indira's untimely death, N.T.R preferred to seek public mandate again, hoping to secure a full majority for himself and went for election again in 1985 March. He won 202 seats in that election and returned to power strongly. N.T.R's close associates in the media fully utilised the advantages of this strong government and amassed wealth in every possible way by pandering to N.T.R's ego. Their wealth and power kept rising, but the needs of the public never came to the forefront.

The Rayalaseema farmers started an agitation with the slogan "13 days, 13 demands, 13 M.L.A.s". Chief Minister N.T.R called them for a discussion at the secretariat on 1st November 1988. N.T.R started from his home for the meeting but stopped his car in the middle of the road and, in the newest spectacle, rested on the middle of the road using his hand towel for over two hours and went back to his home after the show.

The papers the next day usually wrote umpteen things about this showmanship by the C.M, but nobody mentioned the 13 M.L.A.s

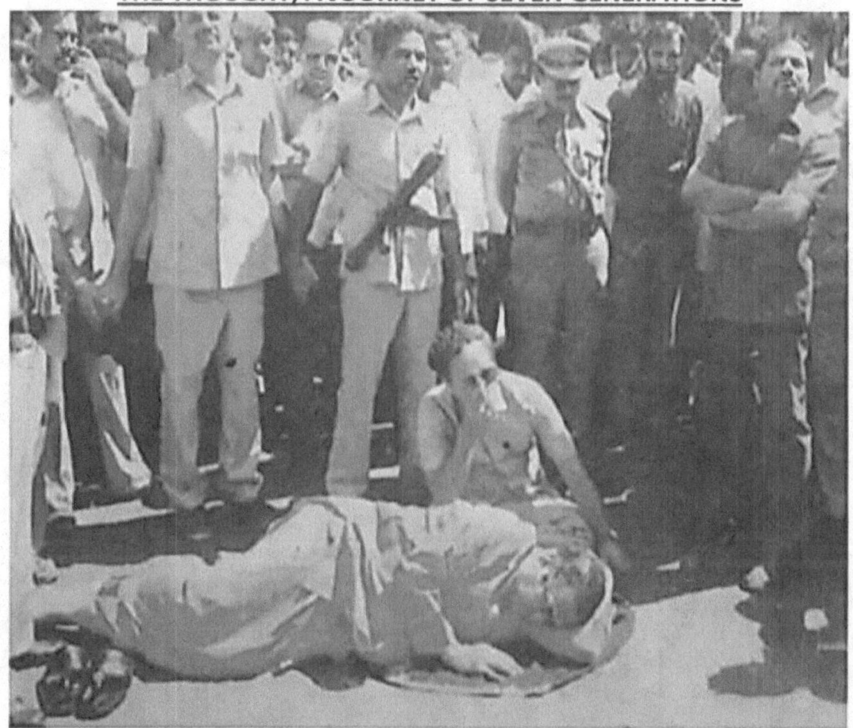

Chief Minister N.T.R political sentiment on the road

and other farmer-leaders waiting at the secretariat for him. After this pass over, the Rayala Seema farmers insisted to take the issue to the centre. The party M.L.A.s resorted to a dharna in front of Rajiv Gandhi's residence in Delhi. They demanded that the Tamil Nadu government settle the Telugu Ganga construction dues of the remaining 52 crores from the total cost of 92 crores. They demanded the right to use the water along the project route. The centre acquiesced to both the demands.

T.D.P had gradually turned into a family party after 1985. Both the sons-in-law were fighting to gain major control in the government and party. Ministers, M.L.A.s and government machinery were crushed between these power centres. The public too was observing all these changes. Few months before the 1989 elections, the entire cabinet was removed, and a new ministry was sworn in. The State had become a hotbed for caste-based violence in this period. Vangaveeti Ranga's murder [98] took place allegedly with Chnadrababu's blessings added to the volatility of the governance in the State. All these factors had an impact on the 1989 elections.

"Is it enough to have media in firm control to secure a good hold over the government permanently?" The events in Andhra during this period proved that it was not so.

Happy Farmer – Homage to Employees

Peketi Nageshwar Reddy, son of Venkata Reddy was born on 20.07.1948, in Kaaja village. After his I.T.I. Draftsmen education, Nageshwara Reddy, took up a job in the Irrigation department in the year 1978. He was part of the quality department in the Nagarjuna Sagar Left canal section first. Between 1985 – 90, he worked on the various phases of the Telugu Ganga Project from Allagadda. After the N.T.R government released a G.O. permitting Rayalaseema farmers to utilise Telugu Ganga project water en route, the farmers were so happy that they organised a big function to felicitate all the project employees, recalled Nageshwar Reddy [99].

Sri Peketi Nageswar Reddy

He later worked at Gannavaram, whose reputation and humility go hand in hand.Mylavaram, Gudivada irrigation department auditing sections. After his retirement, he advised as a consultant on various lift irrigation projects. He is a typical humble Pakanati stalwart

The Only Man in Indira's Cabinet is Indira Herself!

Born Indira Priyadarshini on 19th November 1917 as the only daughter to Jawaharlal Nehru and Kamala Nehru, Indira became the second member of Nehru's family to become the Prime Minister of India. After her initial education in Allahabad, she finished her matriculation from Pune, studied at Rabindranath Tagore's ShanthiNikethan and London's Oxford University. She fell in love with a friend, journalist Feroze in

Smt.Indira Gandhi

Londo n and married him later with the support of Mahatma Gandhi, despite Nehru's opposition to their marriage.

Indira and Feroze's marriage was never amicable, as there were lots of ego issues between them. Due to constant quarrels with the husband, she left Allahabad with both her kids and joined her father, Nehru, in Delhi. In the first-ever general elections in the country, Feroze contested against Nehru from the Rae Baraeli constituency. Indira campaigned on her father's behalf at that time. After Nehru died in 1964, party elders suggested Indira to contest from father's Rae Baraeli constituency. But she chose to take the Rajya Sabha route to enter Parliament as she felt that the recent China war debacle could have a negative impact on her choices. She worked as the Information and Broadcasting minister in Lal Bahadur Shastri's cabinet (1964 – 66). After Shastri's death under mysterious circumstances in Tashkent, Indira became the Prime Minister, though still being a Rajya Sabha MP. She later worked as the PM four times.

Power brings lots of changes to a person's psyche. There is a sort of intoxication in power that blinds persons in the chair to many other things around them. People around them also sing about their greatness so much that they would lose any perception of reality soon. Indira was described as the 'lone man' in the entire cabinet. She encouraged groupism at state level so much that any Congress CM was never comfortable in his seat. They had to run around Delhi for all issues and for Indira's blessings all the time. This has resulted in the lack of formidable leadership in the party after Indira herself. Thus Indira was the top and only leader in Congress. It rose to a level where Indira was India, and India was Indira!

Due to her autocratic nature, she hardly had any regard for other constitutional bodies. Such ego has finally led to the imposition of a national Emergency for 21 months in the country[100].There was not even a single new irrigation project in the entire country during Indira's period! She seems to have no regard for any issues of the farmer's community.

Indian political leadership has become so narrow-minded that they are always worried about their image and would never give any credit to any good work by others. If a previous government has implemented a good scheme, it would be immediately discontinued by the new incumbent. A new project started by the earlier government would not be completed by the present government lest the previous government get any credit. Such selfish, egoistic people have created many problems in this vast country.

Something similar happened in Indira's government in 1980. She put aside the rivers linkage plan and took up "The Green Revolution" across the country. To realise this, farmers were encouraged to use fertilisers and pesticides excessively to increase yield. The yield increased, and the agricultural practices have changed entirely, but the cancer menace has slowly spread across the country due to excessive use of pesticides, fungicides etc.

In the bifurcation of the country, the Punjab region was the most affected as a major part of Punjab was merged with Pakistan. Punjab's then capital Lahore had become a part of Pakistan. East Punjab had no proper capital since then. The creation of linguistic states that began with Andhra Pradesh has brought new problems for the Punjab region. Nehru created a new Punjab State by adding Patiala and other places to the existing unit in 1956.

Akali Dal is a party dedicated to Sikh issues. Akali Dal opposed the creation of the new Punjab and started agitation against it. Master Tara Singh, Fateh Singh and others played a major role in these activities. Indira Gandhi, as PM, has separated part of South East Punjab based on the presence of Hindi speaking public and created Haryana. The city of Chandigarh that was in the middle of both the states was declared to be the combined capital for both states. Few other Punjabi districts were merged with Himachal Pradesh. Sikhs were further aggravated by this division.

Indira used Jarnail Singh Bhindranwale against the Akali forces during their political fight. Soon Bhindranwale became too big a force to be under Indira's beck and call. He proposed a new country for the Sikhs! The Khalistan movement took birth. Pakistan immediately took up this issue to use it for its own political advantage and supported the Khalistan fighters fully. Retired Major General Shabeg Singh, who was part of the Bangladesh Liberation fight, joined with Bhindranwale and started to train the Khalistani's with the Golden Temple as their main centre.

All attempts at truce by Home Minister P.V Narasimha Rao failed. Indira declared "Operation Bluestar" to rid Golden Temple of all the Khalistani separatists[101]. 13 war tanks took part in the operation, and the gates of the Golden temple were blasted off. In the ensuing mayhem, thousands lost their lives; if 500 of them were soldiers, over 3000 were general public! This created permanent rancour in the hearts of Sikhs for Indira and Congress. Intelligence warned of great danger to Indira's life from these emotionally hurt, injured soldiers.

Biant Singh and Satvant Singh were part of Indira's personal security detail for a long time. On 31st October 1984, they shot 23 rounds on Indira to kill her brutally and surrendered, declaring it as an act of retaliation for Operation Bluestar.

Security is generally expected to protect the life of a person. But when they train their guns on the life they are bound to protect, what can anybody do? What ensued was further violence and brutal attack on all Sikhs across North India. Under the directions and support of their leaders, Congress party ranks killed over 3,500 Sikhs and destroyed the lives of countless other families.

All this was a result of a lack of maturity in people to 'stop' something wrong.

Neelam Sanjiva Reddy – the Wise

Sri Neelam Sanjeeva Reddy

The Janatha Party wave swept through the country in the 1977 general elections. It would be difficult to say if it was Indira Gandhi's loss or Janatha Party's victory. Indira established a unique record as a PM who lost in the subsequent elections. Neelam Sanjiva Reddy won from the Nandyal Loksabha constituency as the lone non-congress candidate and was elected the speaker of the 6th Lok Sabha unanimously. Later he was elected as the President of the country, again unanimously, after resigning from the speaker post.

He was the speaker in the 5th Lok Sabha term also; he contested for the President's post as a Congress nominee then. Another contestant V.V. Giri also claimed that he has Congress support. It was Indira's political game that led to Sanjiva Reddy's loss in that election. She gave a call to Congress M.P.s to vote as their conscience told them, which, in other words, was to jettison Sanjiva Reddy.

Thus, V.V. Giri, who took up the President's post at the mercy of Indira Gandhi, signed on to impose an Emergency in the country; agreed to change the constitution 44 times during the emergency and acquired the dubious distinction of being Indira's rubber stamp. After losing that election, Sanjiva Reddy graciously stayed away from active politics, returned to his native Anantapuram and engaged himself in agriculture.

Puritipati Ramireddy of Dokiparru, who was working as a Hindi Bhasha Pandit at Shamshabad, went to Delhi on President Sanjiva Reddy's call and worked as his personal assistant and translator[102]. His simplicity, honesty and humility kept him close to the President's family for a long. He remained in Delhi with Sanjiva Reddy till the completion of his term as the President.

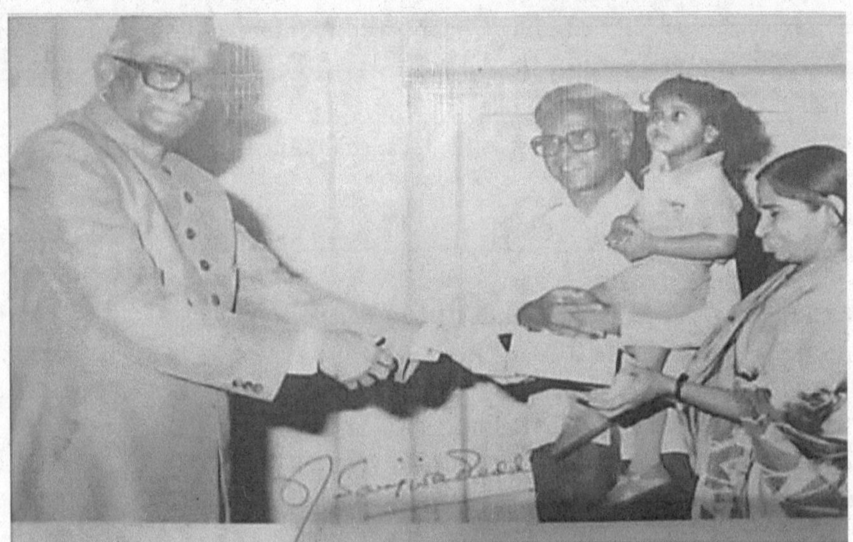

**The family of Sri Puritipati Rami Reddy at the Rashtrapati
Bhavan with President Neelam Sanjeeva Reddy**

***

Water always flows downstream

When problems surround a person completely and continuously, all the relief they can get is when they are able to tell about them to some kind, listening heart. If such friendly sharing doesn't happen, the weight of the problems becomes too heavy a burden. If the person thinks that such sharing might reduce their social image, they should at least have the confidence to gather their strength around them always. Mrs. Bhadramma was never ready to compromise her ego, yet she was ready to risk anything to improve her situation than to lead a life of status quo. She always stayed in a positive mental space and encouraged herself to march ahead.

Such daring always yields positive results. Gold has to take so much beating before it turns into a beautiful, costly ornament. Likewise, hardships usually strengthen a person to handle life better. And any period of hardship cannot last forever, as life is but a cycle of different phases.

Because of all the problems in his life, P.P Reddy's education stopped within Dokiparru school. All the agitations in Andhra Pradesh around that time also forced him to take up farming and support his family. For some time, he worked at R.B. Shastri's Candles Factory at Vijayawada.

Regardless of the problems around him, P.P Reddy was always observant of things around him and was searching for ways to get ahead in life. With his mother's blessings, he decided to migrate to Hyderabad and took up a job at Balanagar in OV Rao's electric pole factory. After gaining some experience there, he ventured into a partnership to handle a few small lift irrigation contract works. The early days of business can be tricky for anybody. More than often, it would be as if treading on a path filled with rocks and potholes. P.P Reddy, too had to face many such impediments and tricky situations in his early days. More than often, he had to wait for the return of his investment despite finishing the job 100%.

P.P Reddy understood the importance of qualifications in irrigations works. Most jobs are allotted to organisations with the right qualifications and ratings. He focused on improving his skill sets and organisational ratings to secure bigger and better contracts.

In the Godavari Basin, the water flow in the river is not at a high altitude from the sea level. But the lands that required the water are at a higher level in comparison. The Godavari flows at 75 - 80 meters level from the sea level. Giving water to Telangana from the Godavari is not a simple task. This is a plateau that is hundreds of meters above sea level. Rayalaseema is also similarly at a higher sea level. So providing water from a lower level river flow to such high places is a huge task.

Telangana's Mahabub Nagar, Rayalaseema's Ananthapur have long since been known as drought areas, famine-stricken lands. Krishna and Penna rivers flow just beside these areas, though at a lower altitude. The poor farmers of these districts thus cannot utilise this water at all. The politicians also went on laying foundations upon foundations, but none of the projects were completed. Shreeshailam Left Canal and Handri-Neeva projects also had several futile starts.

In these conditions, the Palamuru farmers are perennially searching for water. Unable to water their fields, their cattle, they end up migrating to other areas looking for livelihood. Slowly it has come to be known as a "district of migrates." They work as mere labour in other far off lands, despite having many acres of land on their names at home.

At a distance of 185 kilometres from Hyderabad, on the border of Karnataka State, villages called Paspula, Murahari Doddi are situated near the Krishna River, Bheema River joining area. This joint is called

Prayaga. It is at 90 feet below sea level. Paspula, Murahari Doddi villages will have to raise the water 100 feet to get them to their lands!

Around 1983, P.P Reddy worked as a small scale contractor in Manikantha Lift Irrigation – 2 projects. He observed there that water need not always flow downwards for it to be made available to farming. He learned during this project at Paspula village that human effort and newer schemes with proper vision could make wonders like lifting water to higher levels possible. Their second attempt at Murahari Doddi also succeeded, giving him more confidence. He finally found his calling. ***"Where your expertise and the needs of the Nation merge, that should be your occupation,"*** decided P.P Reddy. He told himself that he would dedicate his life to irrigation jobs and would make water available to more and more fields and farmers from here onwards.

This was a realisation and vow that would have a great impact on the future of this region! His march into the future has begun!

<u>The Gift I Could Give My Mother</u>

P.P Reddy started looking at river water like liquid gold. If this water reaches all corners of the earth, what it would yield is nothing less than gold, he thought. And he took it upon himself to go wherever his work took him to realise this dream. Once his objective became clear to him, he transformed into a new man entirely. His approach to looking at things, his grasp, his eagerness, zeal and all other physical and mental faculties changed to aid him in his new tasks. As he was achieving minor targets on the path, the success also began giving him new confidence and happiness.

His mother, Bhadramma, also was able to see all these changes in her son. What else could give more happiness to a mother than seeing her child turn exactly into the person she was dreaming of? Bhadramma's major desire in life was finally fulfilled.

Rivers do not know politics

After taking up the mantle as the CM in 1964, Kasu Brahmananda Reddy played an instrumental role in the establishment of major organisations like BHEL, IDPL, ECIL, B.D.L., Hindustan Cables, Vizag Steel Plant and others in the State. He created facilities and an environment for industrial manufacturing, which lead to the development of many industries here. He resigned from the CM's post in 1971 after the Telangana agitation. In 1974, he became the Central Home, Industries and Communications portfolios minister. In 1977 he became the President of the Congress Party. During his tenure, on 1st January 1978, he took the extreme step of rusticating Indira Gandhi from the Congress party.

Due to his various measures, including the setup of BHEL in Balanagar, many small and big industrial firms mushroomed around the area. P.P Reddy, too set up "Megha Engineering Private Limited," named after his youngest daughter in 1989, in three sheds. He started manufacturing pipes suitable to be used in small scale irrigation and water lifting schemes. He took up contracts in the irrigation and water supply departments regularly, supporting his own industry.

P.P Reddy started going against the saying that "water flows downside only" with his Megha Engineering, using the newer technologies in Hydrology. His belief in technology and desire to satisfy the needs of the public made him work with the belief that "Water Flows Wherever You Take It!"

Fruit-laden Tree

The discipline of P.P Reddy cautions some watchers, while some others feel threatened by it. The sounds of iron arches and welding ark lamp lights are reverberating in the Megha factory. Busy workers running around with their instruments have turned it into sight of a festival for work minded people.

Making pipes is a skilled, yet risky job. While making an iron pipe, it has to be lifted up straight to weld at the spots the fitter has marked. Reaching up to that height itself looks like a daring act. Imagine working with the sparks of welding falling all around! Workers routinely walk on 4-inch, 6-inch width arches at the height of 10 to 50 feet. The onlookers get scared with their daring, but they hardly show any special awareness of the risk. When pipes of small diameters are being made, they are filled with sand and burnt till they are red hot and then twisted to make the required bend. The difficulty in the act has to be seen to believe. Outsiders are hardly aware of these operational issues. People working in these fields find it fascinating.

Sometimes, big 'U' shaped tubes need to be built at 10 feet and lifted up to 30 feet to fix it up. This is a highly complex job. All fitters on the site first build a 'U' tube of one feet diameter. Another team would lift it up using a pulley. After it reaches the required height, fitters and welders work together to attach it as planned.

There are different kinds of jobs in a factory needing different skill sets. The management has to constantly strive, oversee and plan, taking care to not leave any gaps in the working place. This dedication not only gives great satisfaction with regard to the output but also meaning and purpose in life. P.P Reddy also learned to constantly upgrade and derive great satisfaction in meeting newer challenges in the chosen field. His hard work and commitment took Megha Engineering to newer heights.

P.P Reddy observed the various methods and tech up-gradation taking place across the world to meet challenges posed by higher altitude places like Rayalaseema and Telangana in the water supply. He adapted all the necessary steps in the Megha Engineering structure to handle irrigation projects better in these areas whenever opportunities came up. But the political leadership of our areas has long been lax in realising the most immediate needs of the public. That's why projects like Bheema, Jurala, Nettempadu, Kalvakurthi etc., have had so many foundation stones but never progressed any step further.

Farmer – Land –Human Being

A farmer is the first casualty in the struggle between humanity's mistakes and nature's retaliation. A farmer is also the protector of the relation between Nature and Human being. After being patient with the continuous mistakes of humanity, nature retaliates on the greediness of humans. Instances of such retaliations have increased these days, suggesting the never satisfying greedy hunger and exploitation of humans.

The hard work of one farmer feeds several mouths. But the needs of this farmer are being neglected for so long. The governments these days are more focused on acquiring weapons that kill people, than support these providing farmers. Poor farmers go on taking loans which become vicious circles that finally overwhelm them and take their lives. The effects of globalisation have changed governments' focus, and this policy-making has wholly rendered the farmer alone away from society. The media, which should directly stand responsible for society, is also content with sensationalising negative news but is not taking a constructive approach. Without any humanity, The headlines have been the below coming from newspapers for the last 30 years.

Poor Farmer Caught in Loan Web Kills Self

Failing Bores Lead to Farmer's Death

Spurious Pesticides Fail on Crops, But Work Fine to Kill the Farmer!

Failing Crop Prices Push a Farmer to Suicide

Due to a lack of proper water resources, farmers have been waging a daily war with circumstances. The governments somehow never tell these farmers to "Grow Quality Product, We Will Support with Loans." The same government will make a lot of noise, "Make Parts for these... Make Soaps, Make toothpaste... Produce Mineral Water... Loans at zero interest, Tax-free on Income, Free land, Free Electricity"... and so on. Did you ever see a provision of a loan to buy a pair of bullocks? Why are the needs of a farmer looked down on by the government?

Between 1995 and 2002, about 12,716 farmers committed suicide in Andhra Pradesh. Countrywide this number exceeds three lakhs. These are just the official numbers; the unofficial estimates would be much higher. Dependence on bore water has increased as better systems to utilise rainwater properly have not been developed. The digging of bores is an unsure method, and it works only once in 15 attempts. But the farmer has to spend on all 15 attempts, usually on borrowed money. Even if one bore gives water, the loans taken on all the bores would keep on mounting. Even today, about 58% of the population is dependent on agriculture. In these difficult circumstances, farmers are losing hope in life itself. Suicide has become a readily available solution to these poor people. Either the media or the political leadership is not in a position to face the questions posed by the farmers.

A single farmer's suicide could have a lasting impact on a generation. The entire family, particularly the wife, will face so many unimaginable problems[103]. The troubles the family was facing would not end with the passing away of the farmer. The debts won't go away. Newer insults get added. Social and psychological standing would be severely impacted.

It is difficult to imagine the plight of a farmer worried about his next meal while this morsel is still in his mouth. The presence of a farmer's life is noted only when he commits suicide. The inherent agreement and trust between a farmer and nature are linked with the availability of water. When this water is not available, how would a farmer trust his own life? The childhood most of us had just about two decades ago has disappeared without a single trace from even the remotest of villages. Our lives today are nowhere linked with nature.

Since 1990, the open market economy systems have gained speed and acceptance. New wealth is getting created. Karnataka, Maharashtra, and Rajasthan have wisely utilised this new wealth for the construction of irrigation projects. Karnataka finished 11 new projects quickly. It has involved several experts and offices of consequence in discussing and helping in raising Alamatti Dam height. It has promulgated new acts negating the old, British era acts to protect its water resources. Karnataka did not hesitate to drag Tamilnadu to the Supreme Court while protecting its rights.

Giving strength to P.P Reddy's readiness to go to any place for the right contracts, the organisation's expertise has also been recognised by institutions and governments from all corners of the country. As the contracts came in, Megha and P.P Reddy went all-around carrying out the work. This has increased their clout, their network of experts and suppliers of all materials, making the job easier every time.

As Megha was going places, the Andhra political leadership continued its displaced interests here. The very useful Jalayagnam scheme lost political backing. The government concocted several false reasons and peddled them in the media. One usual reason was blaming the erstwhile governments for all the problems, including the poor water availability for farmers. In the Telangana area of the Krishna – Godavari basin, the Master Plan estimates the possibility for 1309 minor irrigation projects. Several of these were promised by different politicians based on political necessities.

But the Polvaram Project started initially as Ramapada Sagar, changed to Indira Sagar, remained languishing in the papers only. Whoever is to be blamed, these incomplete or stalled projects have only lead to the suicides of the poor farmers.

25th August 1995, the Telugu Desham Party formed by N.T.R broke into two factions. N.T.R could not secure enough for his faction, finally leading to his resignation from the CM seat after a week's struggle. Chandrababu Naidu became the CM for the first time in September 1995. His stint continued another term after the 1999 elections. Strangely, Babu's rule was plagued mainly by conditions of famine. His administration also did not spare any thought for improving the farmers' lot.

An agrarian economy, Andhra Pradesh completely disregarded this field and went behind wrong priorities for a long time. The economy was riddled with loans. The suicides of farmers continued, but the state government turned a complete blind eye. Schemes like harvesting pits and groundwater increasing plans were given lots of funds. But schemes for improving surface water availability and distribution were forgotten entirely.

CM Chandrababu commented that "If the government announces ex gratia to the families of farmers who committed suicides, then more farmers would be encouraged to take that route." This holds a big mirror to the lopsided understanding he had in handling the problem! After a foundation laying ceremony, Polavaram was not looked at again in the next nine years! Babu did not even focus on utilising the water allocated by the Bachavat Tribunal. About 40 projects in the Godavari basin got stalled.

All these administrative failures created discontent in public for the party in power. A trend for a negative vote for the incumbent government formed strongly in public.

Regardless of the mood of the general public, the media continued to sing Babu's song. Whatever it may be, media management or control, the most powerful tool used by Babu, failed to represent the larger public opinion. The 2004 election results were a big testimony to this fact.

⁕⁕⁕

<u>The Ambition Fullfilled</u>

They say that luck always favours the brave. The mainly agriculture-focused Pakanati society slowly started venturing towards business. As first-generation entrepreneurs, they tread very cautiously in this new area to minimise losses. It is generally said that in business if you start with money, you will gain experience; if you start with experience, you earn money. But due to the very cautious and prudent approach the early Pakanati businessmen took, they went leaps and bounds constantly.

After Puritipati Venkata Krishna Reddy entered the irrigation sector, he had to make many adjustments with himself and also the society around him. These compromises, necessitated by the circumstances, added to his strength, and he transformed into "Megha Krishna Reddy" eventually. Megha Krishna Reddy explains his own evolution this way:

> *Imagine a person being chased by a tiger. He runs and runs and falls into a valley. Manages to catch hold of a branch of a mango tree that has spread into the valley. As this person is thanking God for saving him, he could hear the branch he is holding breaking. As he could imagine what was about to happen, he saw a ripe mango near him on the branch. He plucked the fruit, took a bite, and found it very sweet. "Wow, how sweet and juicy this fruit is," he exclaimed. If he could enjoy that fruit under the circumstances, that means he is very much living in the present and is clear about having a steady mind. Such unwavering focus is hard to come by.*

> ***If a person feels that he is finished now, nothing can save him. Instead, if he thinks that this is where my life really starts, then he is bound to find new ways. Whatever happens, we are the umpires of our own life. If we say 'out', then it is out. Otherwise, it is not. Our decision is final."***

Megha Krishna Reddy's Observations on Business Issues [104]

"*Something that we don't like is difficult to us. Business is like venturing into a new, unknown area without a tour guide. The present world is in a constant redesigning mode. Everybody is expecting the best products. Whether it is a product or a service, anything of inferior quality is not tolerated. If you are ready to give the best to the world, the entire world will come to you. The entire market will be yours. If changes come in your business like a small stream, it is ok to swim*

Sri P.V Krishna Reddy

against it. But if that change is coming like a big wave, it is pragmatic to go along with it. Life keeps changing. Change is the ultimate law of life. One thing that doesn't suit business at all is "hesitancy." It is an emotion that makes you kill your business with your own hands. When you want to say "NO", never say "YES." Such hesitation and coercion will never make you a great businessman.

If your organisation is able to function smoothly, then it means that your actions and emotions are very much in your control. What you do today will turn into your results tomorrow. You may not see any results today, but if you continue to seed with discipline and strive diligently,

good results will follow. Victory within a day is just fiction. All your failures can be looked at as valuable lessons in experience to reassess the targets of your business. Luck cannot change your business life. Victory will come only based on the scale of your thinking and the follow up by the people around you.

This thinking can be at three levels mainly....

1) Living
2) Winning
3) Ultimate Satisfaction

Youth today have to be mentally very strong to create any wealth. Strict discipline is also a must. Any creation stems first from your own thought. Then only it will take shape outside. The quality of your product can be assessed based on how you treat others around you.

'Do not judge me by my successes; judge me by how many times I fell down and got back up again.'

---- Nelson Mandela

The Ultra-Rich

The most famous institution builders of the Pakanati clan are the pioneering founder of Megha Engineering, Pamireddy Pitchi Reddy(P.P Reddy) and the executive excellence of his nephew Puritipati Venkata Krishna Reddy. Both are natives of Dokiparru village.

Megha Krishna Reddy has been a dreamer who constantly assessed and renewed the targets of Megha Engineering as a socially responsible, modern infrastructure company. He brought a new kind of vitality, vigour and approach to Megha after the solid start given by P.P Reddy. MEIL presently has its feet so firmly in the future that it is hard to see the shades of its own early days in the present structure. Krishna

Reddy has revolutionised the organisation's function, constantly expanding the vision of founder P.P Reddy and is giving it an evolutionary path that is amazing to even dream. Yet, the organisation is firmly rooted in the ethical, moral business practices established by the founder.

Krishna Reddy hardly looks at the position of a person while listening to them and is ready to take a good suggestion from any cadre. MEIL has so far carried out irrigation and water supply projects in 17 states of the country. Every project has been completed within time and as per specifications and standards that benefit the farmer's community the best. As descendants of a farmer's family, what more can these sons of farmers do?

Any organisation mainly has two kinds of assets

   1) **Visible Assets,**
   2) **Invisible Assets**

The clearly visible asset of an organisation is the wealth it has accumulated. The Invisible asset is its knowledge. Both these assets together have lifted P.P Reddy and Krishna Reddy to these astronomical heights. These ultra-rich are not the regular rich we get to see in this world. They firmly believe that there is enough wealth in this world for the entire population. This mindset believing in global abundance is their unique characteristic. They share their riches and accolades judiciously. Finding space in the Forbes Riches List constantly from

2017, the wealth they have accumulated is insignificant before the value they have generated for themselves and the country.

Money itself doesn't turn a person good or bad. But it brings out the inner nature of a person. If a good person's genuine contribution to the world has to happen, it will need money support. Finding and running global level organisations is not as easy as giving lectures and talks about them. To the thousands of employees and indirect beneficiaries of organisations of this magnitude, the founders are nothing less than a god. Looking at the taxes they are paying and contributing to the larger society thus, and they are angels in disguise to many more.

In the context of the successful completion of the Kaleswaram project, Megha chariot riders

The Logical Business Lessons of the Pakanati's

The significant characteristics needed to establish and run a successful business:

1) Audacity
2) Daring
3) Leadership

Audacity

If you are working in a small position for small pay, yet your dreams are always big; it means you are an audacious person ready to take big steps in life. But if the thought process needed for these big steps is not so serious, you will limit yourself to daydreaming and acts like buying lotteries. You have to strengthen your thoughts. If your dreams of big business are strong, you should first calculate your own strengths and weaknesses. Your audacity should first push you to understand yourself better and clearly. This will lead to getting full clarity about the product or service you are planning to start. This will lead you on the right path towards realising it. Life is like a big treasure; to find and grab it, you have to be audacious.

Do not be in a hurry to realise all your desires immediately; learn to be patient enough to plan to realise them. Internal discipline is the only way to greatness. When you affix yourself to a great task, it will bring out your innermost hidden strengths. We cannot change any events in life, but we can always change how we respond to them, leading to positive results. Stop looking for opportunities and start searching for problems. Realise that the treasure of opportunities lies around problems.

True victory in business comes after achieving two things: one, when you fulfil all the requirements of others; two, when you can transform your organisation entirely based on your hard work. Big victories are possible only when you are attentive all the time. The role of hard work in victory is only 20%; the remaining 80% is dependent on how you respond to situations. Reacting is something everybody does; responding cautiously is what makes a great organisation.

Incidents in Business + Response of the organisation = Organisation's Result

Daring

Daring is the biggest inner wealth a person can have. It is wrong to assume that this daring is proportionate to the riches a person has accumulated. The wealth of daring follows you everywhere, unlike any other kind of wealth. Four kinds of daring really help a businessman in making him stand out from the herd he is surrounded by.

1) **Dare to dream,**
2) **Dare to focus on targets,**
3) **Dare to believe in own capacity,**
4) **Dare to live according to global rules.**

Timing is an all-powerful wave in business. One can ride on this strong wave only when one has full belief and readiness in jumping ahead for the targets. If your inner soul is giving you a positive call to jump ahead, believe and take the leap. Your belief will remove all the hindrances in your path and take you ahead.

Business is like a global market clash between many warriors at the same time, where each fight at their full capacity. Big organisations always look like they are on the brink of a precipice, but accomplished businessmen always relish these challenges. When they are faced with an insurmountable offence, real businessmen become stronger. So, be always ready for competition and pressure in business.

Leadership

Leadership is a ritual you perform to realise yourself. The universe is always neutral. Whoever is more ready to take over, the leadership becomes his. This leadership is always dependent on results, not big names. Whoever thinks of crushing others for their own growth will find it hard even to survive here. Business ethics always lead the conscious to the right destination acting like a true compass. Leadership is the ability to show the path, assign roles, command duties, take people along, maintain and control trust, and supervise all aspects of an organisation's different components.

Megha's Philanthropy

We have all read about the kind and big hearts of Karna, Bali Chakravarti, Shibi Chakravarti etc. We also know that many billionaires who make tall claims of their wealth and success fall behind when it is time to return some of it to society. The Pakanati rich society is entirely opposite to this. Their philanthropy is not focused on figuring in the newspapers or to be appreciated by the multitudes. They carry out all their philanthropic activity to bring some change in lives, help the needy, and leave it at that. The generosity to give to others is a trait that develops when the mind reaches the ultimate transformation as a human. Thinking about others, helping the needy, giving back to society, doing a bit for the world we are living in… P.P Reddy, Krishna Reddy's names come foremost to all Pakanati people when they think about these qualities.

Whatever amount of wealth one accumulates, it does not go with him when he dies. The opportunity to do some good to others comes like a rare opportunity generally. To be in the capacity to do so is another fortune altogether. The Megha Contribution to society is at a level that stands as an example to future generations. A mere cursory look at their kind acts shows…

In the entire villages of Dokiparru, Kaza, Jamulapalli, and Narsingapuram, MEIL has established drinking water plants and is supplying hygienic, potable water to all for free. This has resulted in improved basic health in this region.

The Construction of "Bhusametha Venkateshwara Swami Temple" in Dokiparru has turned the village into a pilgrimage site. Marriage halls have been built in Pakanati villages for the use of the public.

Bhusametha Venkateshwara Swami Temple, Dokiparru

Spreading their horizon, they have adopted tens of villages in Karnataka and Telangana and provided basic infrastructure to bring dramatic changes in people's lives.

MEIL has contributed to the renovation and modernisation of the Oncology block in Nizams Institute of Medical Science. They have donated to build a block in the Anantapuram General Hospital.

In Hyderabad's Niloufer Children's Hospital, in Siddhipet and Bodhan Market Yards, under a scheme titled "Bhojanamrutam", over 10 lakh people are provided meals at no cost. This huge act of generosity has been going on for many years. Through "Praanam Voluntary Organization", they donate and serve orphans and patients of AIDS. Respecting their desire to keep their service activity unnamed, I stop here from further listing their charity efforts. I have to exclaim, though, that the Pakanati Legends have already done commendable work for society, with so many other charity plans going on at any given time.

References

86. Yaddanapudi, Baburao. Prehistory of Divisima. Page iii.

87. Dr. Mandali Buddhaprasad, A.B.N. Andhra Jyoti, 18th November 2017

88. Mandale Aadarsam: Tamil Nadu Governor Roshaiya, 5th August 2015, Andhra Jyoti

89. Times of India Article, Aug31st,2004

    http://timesofindia.indiatimes.com/articleshow/833065.cms

90. Interview with Sri Oleti Rami Reddy

91. Nadendla regrets the establishment of T.D.P. Hindu Paper Article 20th January 2003

92. Hariramjogaiya Announcement, Zameen Raitu Magazine. Page 1, 09th March 1984.

93. Today"s affair. Zameen Raitu magazine. Page1, 06th April 1984

94. Indira Gandhi"s speech at the Medak meeting, Zameen magazine. Page 1, 27th July 1984

95. Interview with Nadandla Bhaskara Rao, former Chief Minister of Andhra Pradesh

    https://www.youtube.com/watch?v=YDIjqM4VaLc, (time: 1:24:39)

96. Chegondi Venkata Hari Rama Jogayya, "My Political Life of Sixty Years." Page: 63

97. Andhra Pradesh, 22nd January 1986, Nandyala Revenue Officer ordered illegal demolition of paddy fields by farmers.

98. Chegondi Venkat Hari Rama Jogayya, "My Political Life of Sixty Years." Page: 72

99. Interview with Peketi Nageswarareddy

100. Snehalatha Reddy Prison Diary, Emergency 1977

101. Ramachandra, cave. "Gati tappina Prajaswamyam." India, post-Gandhi (Telugu translation) pages. 576–591.

102. Interview details of Acharya Sri Lakshmi, daughter of Sri Puritipati Rami Reddy Garu

103. Kota Neelima Ph.D. "Widows of Vidarbha" book. Vijayawada. Page: 30

104. Megha Engineering & Infrastructure Head, Krishna Reddy's interview in "Cheppalanivundi." Episode 82 || Cheppalani Vundi E-TV

    https://www.youtube.com/watch?v=lpX0Ydt7-F8

105. Article: 7 Leadership Qualities, Attributes & Characteristics Of Good Leaders, Author: Brian Tracy, Publisher Name, Brian Tracy International

DREAM REALISED

The governments in our State have not concentrated much on any new projects between 1983 and 2004. The only project in this period was the Telugu Ganga Project, envisioned by NT Rama Rao. The needs for water by farmers were hardly cared about during this time. The contractors working in the irrigation and water supply jobs never worried about official scrutiny as there was hardly any.

Eligibility of Contractors: Views of the Society

Even though named 'always truthful', these contractors are never really qualified to handle the work they take up. They hardly care about the quality of the work. These contractors are mere lobbyists who use their closeness to politicians to get big contracts and swindle money out of them. They would satisfy all the demands of the persons in the chair to get these contracts. They would fight among themselves to get them. Even if they resort to fisticuffs or getting the clothes torn, all they are bothered about is getting the contract finally.

At the same time, some other contractors, though fully eligible and known for quality work, just stand aside and watch the entire fracas as they find it demeaning to enter this kind of muck. They would enter the fray, and silently watch when some other heavy-heeled person comes and crushes people all around, and takes away the work. This contract would promptly be thrown to subcontractors who would hardly have any focus on quality. Profit is the only motive, and sooner they get it, the better. Finally, the farmers conclude that all contractors are selfish, dishonest persons.

Even our media has also become a central part of the business. Almost all the profit craze persons have entered here also. If we even think of opposing their writings, they would throw some mud on us to refrain us from speaking. They are never really bothered about this mud themselves, as it is only mud all around them!

When the poor farmers are facing so many issues, it is the duty of media houses to stand for them and write facts regardless of who is on the other side. But this is not happening. Our media is busy campaigning for people who resemble the Republicans and Democrats of America.

You are always alone while chasing your targets

Doing something others have already done, reaching the standards others have already set, is the mindset of the old days. Megha Engineering has focused entirely on the future and did several projects in Karnataka, Rajasthan, Madhya Pradesh, and Gujarat successfully. Due to the abilities and capacity built carefully over the years, these projects were all finished within time and proper standards. This ability has become a habit to them, while it could be a lifelong dream for others.

Who are you? What do you have? Where are you? What are you doing, and how? Etc., questions become very small when you have clarity in "What you are thinking?" It will lead to all the development in your life. Only such people who have a mature answer to this question can lead this world ahead into the future.

Answer Every Call

Megha Krishna Reddy made it a habit to analyse the events and experiences of each ongoing project and plan and prepare for all contingencies in the upcoming projects with due diligence. He would never lose his equanimity, even during the most tumultuous times. He never stopped learning and observing the upcoming technologies in the Hydrology field and was watchful about the new research in the area to include new technology in the projects. He always attended calls, tenders for work from all corners of the country, never ignoring any request, so that he does his bit for taking the country forward in the chosen field.

India is a subcontinent with varied cultural practices, geographical specificities that require unique plans for each project. Over time, Megha specialised in addressing these different needs so that projects grew up and run smoothly like no other organisations could handle. The blockades, loopholes, and bottlenecks in the contract jobs of projects in each area also were thoroughly understood by the Company, and plans to prevent them were in place beforehand. One such measure Megha introduced was to take up the operational maintenance of projects for few initial years themselves. This would bring down lots of worries for the contractee, but as Krishan Reddy was sure about the quality he maintained, it would not be so worrisome to him; rather, it would add greatly to the organisation's image.

As the organisation went on to master the technology and all other components of the job, the command put it in a different level of comfort and negotiation.

Hi-Tech Vision

Nara Chandra Babu Naidu is a man of unique vision, technical command, and stronghold over every aspect of governance among the many contemporary political leaders. But, along with his hi-tech vision, if he had a human angle that could see the necessity of agriculture and the field's problems, he would have set a different standard for future leaders.

It is as if the Telugu political leadership had completely lost any touch with humanity. It is as if humanity itself prayed, begged, pleaded with Chandrababu, yet he turned deaf ears to it! He went on to proclaim that there is no need to study humanities! He declared that days of agriculture are gone, and it is I.T. that is going to rule the world henceforth. But would I.T. produce the food grains needed for the entire world?

Farmer's Pain; Theories

More than the common man, a politician is driven by emotions like anger, desire, greed, sorrow, etc. These emotions drive them towards big positions like chief minister and other seats of power.

Rajashekhara Reddy also worked with the singular desire to occupy the CM's position in the State. He was dubbed a rookie, non-conformist, angry, big-mouthed faction leader. Congress party itself is always filled with many internal squabbles. By 2004, nobody in the State, including Congress leaders, believed that the party had a chance to assume power.

But Rajashekhara Reddy had a singular focus to grab the power, sit on the CM's chair, and start his Long March on 09.04.2003 from Chevella town. He walked several kilometres every day, met villagers, town people, farmers, tourists, labourers, and so on the route, spoke to all of them to understand the needs of the public. After few days of walk, his earlier focus on CM's chair disappeared, a desire to understand the grassroots citizen and to become one of them rose. He felt that he was probably born for just this calling. He was getting to understand the majority of India's agrarian society problems, and he was also getting an idea of how to alleviate their concerns. Soon, addressing the issues of the farming community became his only purpose and desire in that tour.

Despite the hardships of the May sun, Rajashekhara Reddy went ahead with the walk. He would get blisters on his feet, sunburn peeling away his skin, he would get dehydrated again and again, the impact of sunstroke draining away all the liquids in his body, rendering him weak; yet he continued his walk. 38 days and at average weather of 45 degrees heat, he walked over 300 kilometres.

His motives changed, his understanding of people changed, his way of talk changed, he became an entirely new man with a new purpose and path in life. Likewise, the poor and hard-working people across the State have also started identifying him as their saviour. They would follow him in thousands in the walk. The walk of this single man became a big spectacle that was hard to ignore.

Rajashekhara Reddy realised that providing water to every bit of arable land is his only priority. He realised that his path to salvation is linked with water. On 17.05.2003, as he was walking towards the Rajamandry Bridge after Kovvuru, the cool breeze from River Godavari caressed him. All the sweat on his face dried up instantly. It was as if Mother Godavari was wiping away his strain and tiredness with its cool hands. He felt an invitation in the murmur of the river flow. He went into the beach, walking towards the water. Undavalli Arun Kumar, who was walking beside him, told him not to enter the water in the midday heat. But Reddy did not even hear him. He went a bit into the water, stood there as the waves were flowing over his ankles. He felt as if the river was trying to tell him something.

Y.S Rajasekhar Reddy's conversation with river Godavari

Rajashekhara Reddy :Salutes to the Mother Godavari!

Godavari :How are you, my son? Working hard for the CM's seat?

Rajashekhara Reddy :That was before I understood the real needs of the public, mother. Now my only desire is to solve all the problems the farmers of Andhra are facing. To achieve this, taking you to the farmers of Rayala Seema is the only way.

Godavari : You are planning as if you have already become the CM of the State. And you are giving over your responsibilities to me!

Rajashekhara Reddy : Once I say something, I will never go back from it, mother. This time too, I won't!

Godavari : In 1953, the then CM Rajagopala Chari saw my real strength from the helicopter above, was shocked, and wondered also... Why are the Andhra people blessed with such wealth? He sulked. But never worked towards starting any projects. In 1986, N.T.R. too witnessed my might once, but to no use again.

Now you are giving assurances, not even a CM yet...?

Rajashekhara Reddy : Believe me, Mother. I will keep my word.

Godavari : So many have come and gone assuring the same... nothing happened...

Rajashekhara Reddy : Maybe because Telangana and Rayala Seema are much above sea level...

Godavari : Stop with your explanations. If you cannot keep up your word, remember, your politics also would be washed away in time...

If you can take me to the lands of all needy farmers, it would be the happiest thing for me. I would salute you that day. Remember your promise.

Rajashekhara Reddy : The Sun is witness to my word, I will follow your command, Mother; Good-Bye!

Akkineni, Farmers' True Friend

Akkineni Bhavani Prasad, son of Raja Gopala Rao, was born on 20.08.1942 at Boddapadu village in Krishna district. His discipline and adherence to time was learnt early in life as an N.C.C. cadet and later as a training inspector in government schools. In 1989, after his retirement, Bhavani Prasad worked full-time, looking after irrigation needs and solving water problems faced by farmers. As the chief secretary of "Farmers Service Society," he used to represent the water needs of farmers to the government officers and ministers. It is due to one of his petitions which led to court scrutiny in issuing permissions to engineering colleges, the then CM Nedurumalli Janardhana Reddy had to resign from his post.

Another CM had brought him to the police station in the middle of the night, threatened him with dire consequences if he doesn't stop speaking out against him so much. But Akkineni never budged from his path of righteousness. In another instance, fighting for farmers opposing the blatant swindle of 12% interest being charged on them by the banks, Akkineni had to spend over 10 lakhs of his own pension money towards legal expenses. This has finally resulted in the reduction of bank interest to 7% finally [106].

Hydrology is the science that studies water resources. Akkineni studied in depth all the rivers and other water sources in Andhra Pradesh, the geological conditions, the nature of different terrains, etc. He used all this knowledge in advising the chief ministers of the State to handle the water problems of the Rayala Seema and Telangana regions. He faced stiff opposition from many politicians while doing this. As he had been meeting many politicians to discuss the water issues, he became close to Y.S.R. gradually.

When Y.S.R. gave a rest to his Long Walk due to sunstroke, he spent every day of that week understanding water issues from Akkineni Prasad. He called many other irrigation experts also to gain a complete understanding of the history and evolution of rivers in the State. After six days of rest, Y.S.R. continued his walk to finally reach Srikakulam after 68 days of walk. In this long march, he saw many suicides of farmers, the reasons behind them, the electricity problems, the problems in banking sector support to agriculture, and many other issues that have been plaguing the farming sector. On 14th May 2014, Y.S Rajashekhara Reddy took oath as the next CM of Andhra Pradesh.

He immediately started implementing all the irrigation projects he deemed necessary across the State. As a result, 86 projects that were languishing without any progress after initiation were restarted. Most of these were lift irrigation projects. He clubbed them all into one scheme called "Jala Yagnam".

As if rejoicing with all the Y.S.R's attempts to create a better water supply for agriculture, nature too responded favourably, and rains were abundant. Unfortunately, such good fortune and spread of greenery across should have made everyone happy; but the leaders of opposition parties were finding it hard to digest.

First took part in a meeting on "Jala Yagnam" in 2004. From left to right, Minister for Heavy and Medium Irrigation, Sri Ponnala Lakshmaiah; C.M Y.S Rajasekhar Reddy; General Secretary, Farmers Service Society, Sri Akkineni Bhavani Prasad and Retired High-Court Judge, Sri. Lakshmana Rao.

A bag of boons – Polavaram Project

Polavaram is a unique project in the entire world. It is the biggest spill-way, technically most advanced construction. It is a multipurpose project that joins the Godavari with River Krishna and addresses several inter-state water issues also at the same time while producing hydroelectricity too.

Way to the Godavari Pushkara Ghat

"Pushkaraalu", is a unique Hindu religious festival dedicated to each river, held at a twelve-year cycle every time. It is considered to be very auspicious to bathe in the particular river during this period. Hindus pay respect to their parents by observing specific rituals on the river banks during these twelve days. During the Godavari Pushkara season, Chandra Babu wanted to conduct it at a never-before-seen scale, hoping that he would make people forget about the Polavaram scam.

The very many religious leaders, gurus we have, also did their bit and suggested a particular time as the most auspicious for all to bathe in the river. The public promptly followed all this advice and thronged the river. There were twenty Pushkara ghats in Rajahmundry. Four were allotted to visiting V.I.Ps. Due to some odd mistake, all the route signs were leading to one particular ghat only that day.   It   was 14.06.2015. That particular ghat was designated for the general public. But the CM and his family were there as a showreel was being filmed to promote the event, which needed to be filmed among the crowd as per the script. The crowds were kept waiting for more than two and half hours as this grand filmmaking was taking place with the CM and his family members. The costly, super hit film director hired to handle this show was doing his best using multiple cameras, cranes, drones and what not; so that this film gets a slot on National Geographic and adds a feather to the cap of the CM's achievements.

The filmmaking was finally declared over. As the dignitaries were leaving the spot, the ghat was opened for the waiting general public. Already waiting and agitated about the passing of the "Auspicious Time," the crowd rushed forward towards the water in the same instant. What resulted was a stampede that killed 35 persons within no time, injured hundreds of others[107]. The reasons for this accident were clear to the general public, but the committee appointed by CM Babu could not find any reasons. "Hunger for publicity is a dangerous drug!"

Public Money

Polavaram is the lifeline for Andhra and also the most prestigious project in the region. In 2013, before the State was to be bifurcated, the Polavaram Project head-works were given to Transtroy Company at a value of 4,054 crores as per Sonia Gandhi's wishes.

All that a goat knows is about its feed! The government gave thousands of crores towards mobilisation advance to Transtroy Company. Showing these contract agreements, Transtroy took a loan of 7,926.01 crores from a 14 bank consortium led by Canara Bank. But there was hardly any progress in the project as time went by. The Company transferred the loan amounts to its own, personal accounts in a gross misuse.

On 30.12.2019, C.B.I. filed a charge sheet on Transtroy, for cheating the bank consortium. There were no accounts for an amount of 2,300 crores, C.B.I. mentioned in the charge sheet. This reputable Company made a grand show of 1,72,42,625/- rupees donation to the Tirumala temple!

Polavaram to Navayuga's Hands

After Rajashekhara Reddy's sudden demise, the Polavaram project works almost stayed standstill for a long time, only to pick up again after Navayuga was given the work in place of Transtroy in 2018. CM Chandrababu dealt with Transtroy strictly, due to which Transtroy made an agreement to hand over the jobs to Navayuga Company[108]. The spillway concrete works were started immediately by Navayuga.

Cofferdam, diaphragm wall, spillway, and other works were started simultaneously. Masood committee that was constituted by the state government to oversee the progress reported that 3,800 cubic meters of concrete works were taking place every day in this new phase. On 06.10.2019, 30 thousand cubic meters of concrete was poured within 24 hours to create a Guinness world record.

New Swing

After YS Jagan Mohan Reddy came to power in the State, the importance to Polavaram increased exponentially, and the speed of work also grew accordingly. Though the contract is in Transtroy's name, the work is done by Navayuga, and the bills are also paid to them unofficially. Due to the complications arising out of this situation, Jagan's government proposed a reverse tendering system.

Under the new method, the government awarded the new contract to Megha Engineering for an under quote of 780 crores. The Polavaram Project was redesigned to handle a peak water flow of 50 lakh cusecs. Megha organised for the newest technology from across the world and with a focused plan, started the work in November 2019.

The world's biggest dam, the Three Gorges in China's spillway capacity, is less than Polavarm's capacity. Being built to handle 50 lakh cusecs flow, at a length of 1.18 kilometres, with 48 hydraulic, radial type gates, with a crust level of 25.72 meters, with a full depth of 45.72 meters which means at least 20 meters of gates stay submerged always.

Full name	Polavaram project
Inauguration	1981, 2004, 2016, 2019
Water assignment	301.38 TMC
Reservoir capacity	194.6 TMC
Strategy	7.20 Lakhs
The length of the main canal	Left canal – 181.50 k.m. Right canal – 174 k.m.
Estimated cost (2020)	47,725.74 Crores
Construction phase	Not done yet

Megha brought a swing to the work with over 8 thousand workers handling the job round the clock to utilise the underflow period for the Godavari between March and June. The pandemic has overturned the world economy quite unexpectedly, Covid-19 has also impacted the Polavaram project. Along with the lockdown imposed countrywide, Megha also stopped all work on the project and relieved the workers so that they could reach their homes safe and within time.

After the lockdown was lifted, the project work was resumed in June. Megha organised special trains to bring back the workers, who are mostly from Bihar and Uttar Pradesh. Due to the planning and foresight of Megha, despite the 22 lakh cusecs water flow of floods in August 2020, the project works were not impacted much.

As per the plans, and the present progress in work, the Polavaram Project could be finished by 2021 December, announced Central Water Works minister Gajendra Shekhawat in the Parliament [109].

Polavaram should not be a water storage dam

Shree Shailam and Nagarjuna Sagar Projects are designed as water storage dams, constructed between hills. Polavaram is being built on sandy shores with a concrete basement at a depth of thousand meters. Godavari flow in this part will be heavy for 120 days. All this floodwater needs to be stored in the right places that are better suited by gravity and better connectivity.

Khammam District	Flooded Villages
Vararamachandrapuram	45
Kunavaram	48
Chinturu	17
Kukkunuru	34
Velerupadu	39
Bhadrachalam	13
Burgampadu	09
West Godavari District	
Polavaram	29
East Godavari District	
Devipatnam	42

These reservoirs should be planned to store water in two tanks at least per Mandal as such storage will increase the groundwater availability in the region. Such planning would also ensure water supply to all arable land across the State. This will benefit the environment also with an equal distribution of resources.

Andhra has to transform into Haritha Andhra, most definitely. But to achieve this, submerging 9 Mandal of forest area in one place is not sensible. Displacing so many tribals, hurting these Adivasis of hills and forests to benefit the people of flatlands is not humane. Forest-dwelling Adivasis are known for a unique oneness with nature. They consider the trees and animals surrounding them a part of their families. Every step of their lives is connected to the plants and plant products. Such unison with nature is hard to achieve and maintain. They gather tamarind, gum, honey, different nuts, leaves, palm products, etc., to maintain their lives. If these simple, nature-dwelling lives are displaced and pushed to live away from their forests, will they survive?

Pushed away from their natural surroundings, can they lead a life of peace and comfort in alien surroundings? It is reported that when these tribals were told that they would be rehabilitated, they asked whether the hills and trees would also be rehabilitated!

Re-allocation of Water is the only solution

The distribution of water should not be on the basis of linguistic states. What is the link between water and language? The criteria should only look into places with water availability and those without. Karnataka woke up to its water needs in the '90s and has been fighting for them since then. That is why the Andhra people have been accusing Karnataka of blocking the flow of water. The politicians of both regions have also been working to cash the issue and public sentiment for political benefits. Karnataka region has already seen enough water wars. Thousands of Tamil families had to flee from erstwhile Karnataka state due to these wars. The Kaveri water issue is still simmering, and the selfish, narrow-minded behaviour of politicians of both regions could cause more wars.

In the epic Ramayana, monkey king Vali was blessed with the unique power to acquire half his opponent's energy in a fight. Using this unique gift, he won over many strong people, including Ravana. Even Rama had to hide behind a tree to hurt him to avoid the effects of this boon.

The state government is saying that shifting Godavari water to the Krishna basin is one of the main targets of the Polavaram Project. As per the Bachavat award, measured to the tune of water shifted from Godavari basin to Krishna basin, we would lose half the amount of water in Krishna water allocation. That means, if 80 T.M.C. of Godavari water is shifted to Krishna basin, Karnataka and Maharashtra would take away 35 T.M.C. of Krishna water and will release only 45 T.M.C. downwards for us. This could create problems for Rayalaseema and Telangana when water availability is less in the Krishna River.

Compared to the coastal belt and Telangana, water resources are less in Rayalaseema. Seema area for long had been neglected in getting proper water for irrigation. Rayalaseema farmers had great hopes for Krishna, Penna water for their irrigation needs, but their needs were unmet. Tamil people along with Seema people have lost their rights over Krishna water.

Rayalaseema is on the way to desertification. The anguish of the people of the region has always been neglected. If the Coastal public agrees to sacrifice their demand for a share in Handri – Neeva, Galeru – Nagari, Veligonda projects, the Seema problems might come down to some extent. A broad-based, human vision is needed to share natural resources like water properly.

Let us accept a reduction in Bachavat award water allocation from 75% to 60%. That would mean, the Krishna district farmers would get water not three out of four years, but three out of five years. If the Sarkar districts accept this proposal, the allotted Krishna water will increase. That would mean we can plan more projects for the increased amount of water. With 60% assurance, we will get another 200 T.M.C. water, which can be allotted to Rayala Seema entirely. This will provide water for 4 lakh acres in the region for dryland crops. Even drinking water needs could also be met with this allocation.

Linking of Rivers

North India Linked Proposals	South India Linked Proposals
Kosi – Mechi	Mahanadi - Dhavalesvaram (G)
Kosi - Ghagra	Inchampalli (G) - Nagarjuna Sagar (K)
Gandak - Ganga	
Ghagra - Yamuna	Inchampalli (G) - Pulichintala ((K))
Sharada - Yamuna	
Yamuna – Rajasthan	Polavaram (G) - Vijayawada ((K)
Rajasthan – Sabarmati	Almatti (K) -Penna
Chunar - Sone Barrage	Srisailam (K) - Penna
Sone Dam - Ganga Link	Nagarjuna Sagar (K) - Somashila (P)
Manas - Sankosh - Tista - Ganga Jogigopa - Tista - Farakka	Somashila (P) - Polar- Kaveri
	Kaveri-Vaigeyi-Gundar
Farakka - Sundarbans	Ken - Betwa
Ganga (Farakka) - Damodar - Subernarekha	Prabati-Kalisind-Chambal
Subernarekha - Mahanadi	Par - Tapi - Narmada
	Thaman Ganga -Pinjal
	Bedti- Warda
	Netravati - Hemavati
	Pamba -Achamkovil -Wippar

INTERLINKING OF RIVERS IN INDIA

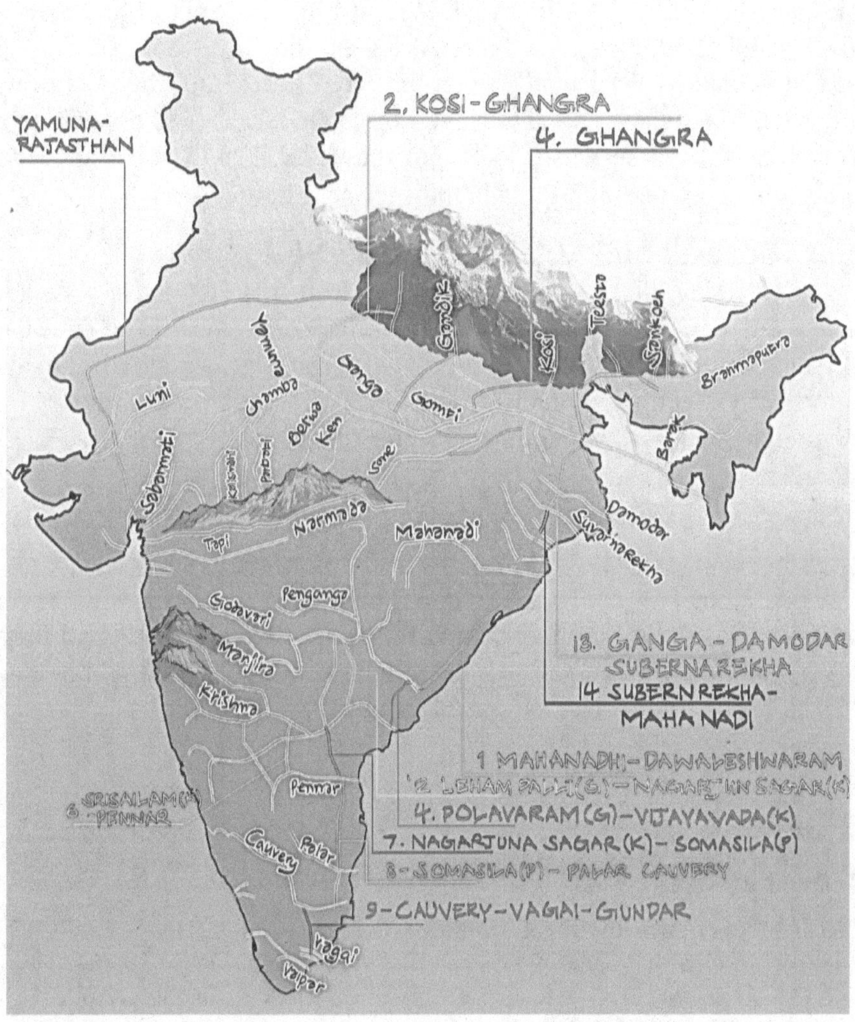

Since the 1970s, plans have been proposed to link 37 rivers, at 39 spots across the country. This was deemed a permanent solution to the disproportionate spread of water resources in the country.

More and more discussions on these proposals made by Dr. K.L Rao and Captain Dinshaw Dastoor should be stopped, and implementation needs to be started at least now. Northern India's

Himalaya region has 14 spots, Central India has 16, and Southern India has 9 spots for these linkages. Ganga and Brahmaputra river waters are subject to international water allocations that need coordination with China and Bangladesh. These can be set right with time and patience. Likewise, the North and South India river linkages will have to deal with the impediment of the Vindhya Range of hills. As South Indian rivers are not linked with any international issues, they are ready to be taken up immediately. Mahanadi water can be shifted to the Godavari; Godavari to Krishna; Penna to Kaveri up to Gundar. Let us hope that the governments will seriously look into these linkages to solve all water problems in entire South India in the very near future.

The Seventh Generation Information

Today, the Seventh Generation Pakanati's are spread wide and across all corners of the world. Few engineering, medicine-educated persons in the Fifth Generation have grown exponentially in the Information Technology arena in the Sixth Generation, and immigration to foreign countries has become a routine thing.

We understand our motherland when we are far from it. Likewise, the Seventh Generation is growing up in a completely new cultural setup now.

I sincerely wish that **"The Thought – A Journey of Seven Generations"** will function as the thread that would connect all these generations together again. I sincerely hope that this book will help us all in continuing to reaffirm our place in history forever.

References

106.	Interview with Sri Akkineni Bhavani Prasad

107.	"Intiperu Indraganti," Srikanth Sharma Autobiography. Page: 415

108.	(i) Andhra Jyoti, Another History in Polavaram, Guinness World

109.	Record, 07th June 2019.

(ii) India Herald, back into Polavaram Navayuga, 16.08.2019

(iii) A.P. 7 A.M., Navayuga entering production, 10th February 2018

110.	Union Water Energy Minister Gajendra Singh Shekhawat's written answer to MP Keshineni Nani's question in 2019

MY JOURNEY THROUGH THE BOOK

For this long journey of mine, the contribution of my teachers who educated me in my childhood, the books I have read, and my thoughts... were helpful until this book was completed. I grew up close with the fourth-generation people in this book with a sense of humanity. It was a beautiful journey through the love and intimacy of a joint family throughout my childhood. As a kid, I used to do a lot of mischiefs and countless mistakes. My family members were tensed about my future. My Education went on with slightly higher marks than average marks. But, since childhood, I have been well accustomed to studying the conditions around me.

I started being friends with the humanity around me from my childhood. Even the teachers, whom I admire, have taught me lessons that have been combined with humanity. Among those teachers, who should be mentioned herein, is Sri Vangivarapu Raghavachari, my Telugu teacher. He taught us a combination of good Telugu lessons and life philosophy lessons, which always contributed to student's psychological development.

With scout trainer Raghavachari teacher, Dokiparru alumni

MY JOURNEY THROUGH THE BOOK

The Telugu Teacher was a pioneer of the scout group at school. He changed the student's enthusiasm into perseverance, patience, and increased sociability. Efforts were made to train students to become community workers. In the process of bringing libraries closer to the students when libraries are available, he promoted the scientific outlook and discernment of the students each year with the help of Nadendla Arjuna Rao, a

Sri Nademdla Arjuna Rao

Librarian. As part of that, patriotic plays with children were organized and programs to train them to become future warriors.

Every year in school, Mock legislature meetings were held to educate students about the practices of the state legislature. In those meetings, I played the role of the State opposition Leader (N.T.R).

Going to libraries and reading books was an addiction for me as I participated in these events with curiosity and joy. This addiction led me to write this book, **"The Thought, A Journey of Seven Generations".**

Pamireddy Suresh
Chandra Reddy

Butchi Reddy, his son, Dr. Suresh Chandra Reddy, has been giving away prizes to students under the title "The Roll of Honor" and helping them to pay more attention to their studies, who scored the highest marks in the seventh and tenth classes of secondary school. In addition, he is encouraging students with attractive prizes who held the best drama, essay, and cursive competitions, etc., in Library activities.

My childhood, which continued in such a friendly atmosphere, laid the foundation for the ideas in this book. When I was eighteen, I first read Gandhi's autobiography, SatyaShodhana. After reading the fact-finding book, I stood upright, realizing the uniqueness of the legacy force and understanding the hard work of previous generations. It struck me for the first time that it was necessary to search with a healthy historical understanding and introduce this history to the next generation as a narrative.

I realized that if we touch the memories of the Telugu people's past and vital events together, that would be our history. This time the consequences of my thought were entirely out of my control. The bet started in me that I would do anything I could.

I have divided the knowledge to write this book into three sections.

1. I know - Things I know

2. I don't know - Things I know

3. Even things I don't know - things I don't know

When I wanted to write the book **"The Thought – A Journey of Seven generations"**, the problem came up with the "Third section".

For the first time, I knew that I was completely unfamiliar with the lifestyle of the first three generations. The only way for me to know about the unknown things was to thoroughly explore and study the pre-history books, genealogies, and events in the Pakanati community one by one. But, in the millions of pages of literature, it isn't easy to find about the Pakanati trend. It was not known who wrote it. Not even sure if it was written or not at all. It is understood that all these steps are in the third section of the above "Even things I don't know - things I don't know".

My intuition is that I need to see new perspectives that have not yet been discovered about the history of Pakanati, and the desire to write had become more stronger.

My journey towards the exploration of Pakanati history started from the State Central Library in Hyderabad. I have read many books on

Telugu history and literature in Library and have taken note of some of the books that have been written about the Pakanati community. Regarding them, I started to search for evidence in the British records too. Initially, I didn't even know if there would be any result with this work or not. But I kept doing it and wrote the notes on the information which I collected.

For British Records, the British Library in Hyderabad was very useful to me. My mind was mainly searching for something else near the WD 1061 OIOC shelf in the Library. Occasionally, I laughed at not knowing what I was doing

Potti Sriramulu University has translated some of McKenzie's documents related to Telugu villages into the Telugu language and embedded them. When I read those records, the information I found was so separate, in the form of events. I have collected and carefully read some of the biographies associated with Pakanati events.

When I was reading 18th-century records as part of literature, it contained Telugu numerals. Learning new Telugu numerals seemed fun to me. Telugu numerals are in our books approximately up to the time of the 1926 novel Malapilla. Gradually English numerals came, and Telugu numerals were not taught in schools either.

One of the documents I have collected here is related to the villages of Dokiparru and Rachuru. But, these were not related to the Pakanati villages. These two villages belong to the villages of the Guntur district, which were south of the river Krishna. Pakanati villages were located north of the river Krishna. As time went on, I perceived that it was much harder to comprehend than to gather information gradually.

In my search for a few days, I knew what to write. While I was confused about how good it is to write, I was fascinated by the Indian language sound 'epic' by Guntur Sheshendra Sharma in his book 'Naa Desam, Naa Prajalau... My Country, My People'. I understand that this book is an ethnography that provides with a particular culture, society. I also perceive how their narrative skill is when telling ethnography. On a day-to-day basis, observing an aerial view of a subject has become a daily task for me, and I have adhered to the principle that the observer should not have any opinion as part of it.

Of the Telugu autobiographies, the ones most available to me are the biographies of the Niyogi Brahmins. They are all from Andhra. Dasu Sri Ramulu, Kandukuri Veeresalingam, Gurajada Apparao, K.L

THE THOUGHT, A JOURNEY OF SEVEN GENERATIONS

Rao, Sonti Venkata Ramuurti, Tanguturi Prakasam, Pamulaparti venkata Narasinhrao (PV), Jiddu KrishnaMurti, Sarvapalli Radha Krishna, Tenali Ramakrishna ... and many more.

Niyogis gave great importance to their history. I have noticed that some mysterious words are used extensively in what they write. The former Prime Minister, P.V.'s autobiographical novel 'Insider' is from this perspective. With this approach, they say what they want to say. Only those who read will understand depending on their level of knowledge. Very few of us have the quality of noticing greatness in our peers. For some, it may not be possible.

Akkiraju Ramapati Rao wrote a critical essay on 'Telugulo aatmakadhalu - Autobiographies in Telugu'. Through this, the first autobiography to be written in English was the autobiography of Vennelakanti Subbarao (1877), thus revealing the flow of thought in the 17th century. If we examine the history of the Kashi Yatra of the Yenugula Veeraswamy, we can understand the culture of the 18th-century, transport, the conditions of the farmers, and the culture in different parts of the country by region.

While they travel from Kashi, they both took shelter at 'Dokiparru- Pakanati inn'. It was written down in their diaries and books. I thought it was the first recognition for my research. With that, little hope sprouted that this research I was doing would yield results.

When I closely examined the East India Company records, Uyyalawada Narasimha Reddy, Gosai Venkanna, Alluri Sitaramaraju, Mallu Dora, and Gantam Dora come to the fore. When I read the manuals of Krishna, Guntur, Godavari, Kadapa, and Kurnool districts, it seemed merely the history books of the Niyogi's as they were written for our village reasons. When I saw the Kurnool manual and came up with the word 'Chenchu', it seemed that it was brazenly talking about Vasireddy Venkatadri Nayudu.

It cannot be said that some British died because of the Chenchus. But the British were so frightened by the word Chenchu. I noticed that the Niyogi's writing went on so wonderfully, without symbolically saying the original thing in those texts, without leaving their subject entirely.

If you read the books written by Sri Kodali Lakshmi Narayana and Sri Gorripati Venkata Subbayya, you will know the life of the zamindars. If you look at the books published by Vignana Chandrika Grantha Mandali, you will know the history of Andhra Pradesh and the situation in India. The lyrics written by Ayyadevara Kaleswara Rao, Digavalli Venkata Sivarao and Vasireddy Durga Sadashiveshwara Prasad are very famous.

If you look at the books written on behalf of the Abhudaya Writers' Association, Srirangam Srinivasa Rao (Sri-Sri - Arasam President) and Tummala Venkataramaiah (Arasam Secretary), I realized that most of the people who took the lead in the struggle for life and led the development of the community came, especially from the middle class.

If "History of the Congress", written by Bhogaraju Pattabhi Sitaramaiah, is shown from the perspective of the higher castes, From the "Hindu castes and sects" written by Jogendranath Bhattacharya in 1896, We can see how the British conspiratorially named and divided us into castes.

Reading 'Life of General Sir Arthur Cotton' reveals the living conditions of the farmers and be able to understand the relationship between humanity and water. If we read the 'Communist Manifesto' by Carl Marx and look at the 'Heigl' theory 'stated by the German philosopher, we will see the role of self-power in the journey of human life, the course of human history changed circumstances and social conflict.

Apart from being for a Ph.D, Bangore (Bandi Gopalreddy), a renowned writer and historian, is truly a great thing to have a history of dedication enough to fit ten PhDs.

Digavalli Venkata Sivarao was a literary warrior, a humble and peace lover, who Fought against the British. He was charged three times by the British with treason under Section 124-A. The entire history of Krishna district independence was included in the diaries of Shivarao, including the names. During his lifetime, his literary work was a significant event. Many historical objects were dug up from nowhere and, with great effort, was brought to light for the Telugu people. He has authored nearly 40 books and 400 articles. They took due care to extract the required information from the bundles of notes written by Shivarao. It is a long-standing habit of him to take notes while reading any book. Thus, the bundles of many notes he practised and wrote history are like a valuable treasure to us.

Dr. Digavalli Ramachandra, the son of Sivarao, helped me with a special interest in the history of these seven generations with a big heart and provided me with what I needed.

<u>**THE THOUGHT, A JOURNEY OF SEVEN GENERATIONS**</u>

If you want to know the exciting events in the history of Andhra, In that case, you need to know a lot about Mallampally Somasekhara Sharma, who has dedicated his entire life to writing historical research.

We find all the regional, national and international events of the last 90 years, including the evidence in the weekly Zameen Raitu paper. The Hindu Paper Archive is also very helpful in this regard. For this, we especially need curiosity and a little patience.

I was born in a peasant family. It seemed to me that someone had asked me to tell the way of life of four Era of a peasant through the book **"The Thought – A Journey of Seven Generations"**.

It felt it's my responsibility to talk about those in the Pakanadu community and pass this seven generations' information to the next generations. In 2011, I decided to give a book form to my thought flow. After coming to Malaysia, it seemed to me that there was still a lot to be done, given the full range of things that had been collected and stored before. I realize that there was research in my work. I began to study for a doctorate as part of a research course at the University of Northern Malaysia. This time the work I was doing began to excite me. As part of data collection, the deep affection for literature has grown this time around.

Applying research methods has become a game. I have no idea why I am reading thousands of pages. But for the final Information Gathering, I kept reading again and again.

I read 18th-century and 19th-century literature in the form of biographies. I approached university professors in the form of questions. As I was closer to the professors with questions, then my task became easier.

I stirred up more than a hundred Pakanaati people with questions. This book is a collection of answers given by them, and I have collected old memories and photographs from the descendants of Pakanati and provided them in this book.

To say greatness is like intoxicating. I think boasting is an extravagant activity of my "I". So I humbly end here, thinking that I only know little. Feel free to share your thoughts on this book. I will correct them in new editions.

MY JOURNEY THROUGH THE BOOK

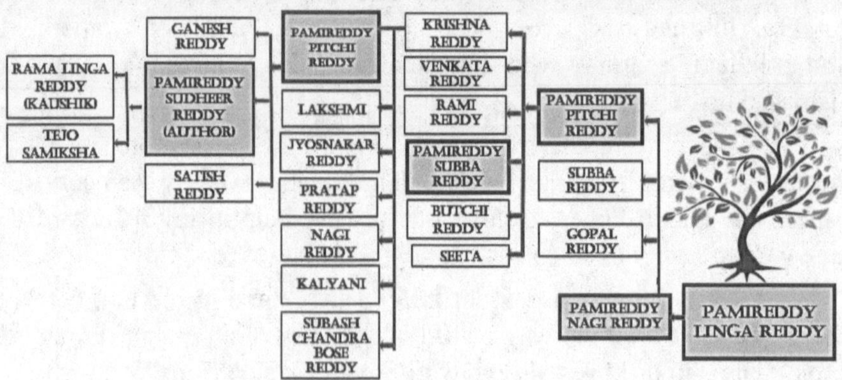

PERSONAL INTERVIEW DETAILS

01. Dr.Kolakaluri Enoch, Ph.D., Retired Vice-Chancellor at S.V. University, SKU University, Hyderabad - 18th,19th-Century Literature.
02. Dr.Darla Venkateswara Rao Ph.D., Professor, Dept. of Telugu, Centrel University, Hyderabad -18th,19th-Century Literature.
03. Dr.Kolakaluri AsaJyothi Ph.D., Retired Telugu Professor, Jnana Bharati Campus, Bangalore University, Bangalore - 18th,19th-Century Literature.
04. Dr.Kolakaluri AsaJyothi Ph.D., Retired Telugu Professor, Jnana Bharati Campus, Bangalore University, Bangalore -18th,19th-Century Literature.
05. Dr.Pamireddy Damodara Reddy Ph.D., Author, Vasavi Degree College Principal /Faculty, Anantapur - 18th,19th-Century Literature.
06. Dr.Kolakaluri Madhujyoti Ph.D., Telugu Professor, Padmavati University, Tirupathi - 18th,19th-Century Literature.
07. Dr. Ginnarapu Adinarayana Ph.D., Telugu Professor, Osmania University, Hyderabad - 18th,19th-Century Literature.
08. Dr.Pamireddy SriLakshmi Ph.D., PDF., Professor, Osmania University, Hyderabad - Pakanati culture and customs.
09. Dr.Ravikiran Kumar Reddy Ph.D., Professor, Ted Rogers School of Management- Ryerson University, Canada - The role of Pakanati in the freedom struggle.
10. Dr.Dasu KesavaRao Ph.D., Retired Hindu Paper Deputy Editor, and Buero Cheif, Hyderabad - 18th,19th-Century Literature, The role of Pakanati in the freedom struggle.
11. Dr.Digavalli RamaChandra Ph.D., Retired, Bank of India, Director, Hyderabad -18th,19th-Century Literature, The role of Pakanati in the freedom struggle.
12. Dr.Achyuta Rao Ph.D., Retired Sr. Scientists, Hyderabad - 18th,19th-Century Literature.
13. Dr.P.Lakshmi Ph.D., Telugu Professor, Hyderabad - 18th,19th-Century Literature, The role of Pakanati in the freedom struggle.
14. Dr.Vangivarapu Navven Kumar Ph.D., Physics Professor, JNTU University, Gudivada - School, and Library in Dokiparru
15. Dr.Vishesh, Author, President, International Association of Neuro-Linguistic Psychology (India), C.E.O. of Genius Gym-Psycho educational Model, Hyderabad - Culture, and Customs.
16. Dr.Pamireddy SivaReddy Ph.D., Retired, Telugu Professor, SKU University, Anantapur., Anantapur - Pakanati culture and customs.
17. Sadmeka Lalita Ph.D., Telugu Assistant Professors, Bellampalli Degree College, BellamPalli - 18th,19th-Century Literature.
18. Dr.Vasubabu Rajulapati Ph.D., Mathematics Professor, Vishnu Engineering College, Bhimavaram - Pakanaati villages
19. Polavarapu Prasanti Ph.D., Social Worker, Hyderabad - Culture and Customs.
20. Sri Lella Kalidas Venkata Ranga Rao, IPS,DIG of Police, Visakapatnam Range.,Visakapatnam - The role of Pakanati in the freedom struggle.

21. Akella Raghavendra, Indian Civil Services Trainer, Author, Educator with mastery of Telugu, Anthropology, Sociology, and Philosophy Hyderabad - 18th,19th-Century Literature.
22. Dr.Rajasekhar, Indian Wikipedia Community, Hyderabad - 18th,19th-Century Literature.
23. Sri Pamireddy Jagadish Chandra Reddy,Isro Senior Scientist,Srihari Kota - Pakanaati villages
24. Sri N.Sudhakar, Indian Oil Employees Union, Secretary, Hyderabad - Pakanaati villages
25. Sri Manda Nagendra Prasad Reddy,Ex.Editional PP Lawyer, Gudivada - Pakanaati villages
26. Sri K.V.B.Sankhar, Retired ONGC Employee, Vijayawada - The role of Pakanati in the freedom struggle.
27. Sri Kanumoori Sesha Sai Praneeth Reddy M.S, Research Assistant, Sorbonne University, Paris, France - Pakanati culture and customs.
28. Dr.P.Suresh ChandraReddy, Jaya Hospital, Pamarru - Pakanaati villages
29. Sri Dukkipaati Kishore, Retired APIDC, Hyderabad - Pakanaati villages
30. Sri Polavarapu Sridhar, Business, Hyderabad - Pakanaati villages
31. Sri Vatrapu Venkata Lakshmi, Housewife, Bangalore - Pakanaati villages
32. Sri Vundi SubbaReddy,Farmer,Dokiparru - Pakanaati villages
33. Sri Puritipaati GangadharaReddy, Redson Industries Pvt Ltd, Hyderabad - The role of Pakanati in the freedom struggle.
34. Sri Kanumoori KotiReddy, Kobashi Machines and Tools Pvt Ltd, Hyderabad - Pakanaati villages
35. Sri Syyad Mastan, Indian Navy, Mumbai - Dokiparru School
36. Sri vundavalli SeshuGopal,Business ,Chennai - Polavaram Project
37. Sri Maddala Venkateswara Rao, Telangana Electricity board Employee, Hyderabad - Dokiparru School
38. Sri Jonnalagadda Krishna Rao, Medical Representative, Vijayawada - Pakanaati villages
39. Sri Puritipaati Satish Reddy, IT Manager, Hyderabad, Pakanaati villages
40. Sri Makireddy PurushottamaReddy, Rayalaseema Intellectuals Forum, Coordinator, Tirupathi - Polavaram Project, Irrigation
41. Srimati Vatrapu Mangamma, Housewife, Farmer leader, Kaza - The role of Pakanati in the freedom struggle.
42. Sri Jonnalagadda Bhaskar, Village priests, Dokiparru - The role of Pakanati in the freedom struggle.
43. Sri Pamireddy Srinivas Reddy, Sales and Marketing Manager, Hyderabad - Pakanaati villages
44. Sri Meduri Srinivasacharyulu, Pasumarru Govt school teachers, Dokiparru - Pakanaati villages
45. Sri M.Kalyan, Business, Hyderabad - Information Resources, Government Records, Legislative, Prison Diaries.
46. Sri Pamireddy VenkataReddy, Retired Centrel Govt. Employee, Hyderabad - Pakanati culture and customs.
47. Sri Pamireddy Venkata Subbarao Reddy, Business, Hyderabad, Hyderabad - The role of Pakanati in the freedom struggle.

48. Sri Veeramachaneni SivaPrasad, Retired K.C.P Employee, Dokiparru - Culture, School, Lakes.
49. Sri Pamireddy Ramireddy, Sales and Marketing Manager, Saudi Arabia - Pakanaati villages.
50. Sri Nadendla Ravikumar, A.P. Ploce Dept, Vijayawada - History of Dokiparru Library.
51. Sri Ravulapaati MurahariReddy, Insurance Agent, Kaza - The role of Pakanati in the freedom struggle.
52. Sri Marrivada VenkatewaraReddy, AP Electrical Engineer, Hyderabad - The role of Pakanati in the freedom struggle.
53. SriPamireddy VenkaReddy, Retired Bhel Employee, Hyderabad - Pakanati culture and customs.
54. Sri Dukkipaati AppaRao,Farmer, Business,Dokiparru - Dokiparru Culture, School, Lakes.
55. Sri Kishore, Retired School Teacher, Gudivada - Dokiparru School
56. Srimati Sarala, Retired School Teacher, Nuziveedu - Dokiparru School
57. Srimati Vijaya Lakshmi, Retired School Teacher, Chennai - Dokiparru School
58. Sri Arige Ashok Babu,IT Manager,Nandaluru,Pakanadu.
59. Sri Vamsi Rahul, IT Manager, Hyderabad - The role of Pakanati in the freedom struggle.
60. Sri Ayoob Beig, School Teacher, Dokiparru - Dokiparru Culture, School, Lakes.
61. Pakanati SubbaReddy,Farmer, Business,Khambam - Pakanaadu
62. Sri Medhuri VijayaSaradhi, Pharmaceutical Manager, Hyderabad - Dokiparru culture, school
63. Sri Vatrapu Srinivas Reddy, Farmer, Business, Kalaparru - The role of Pakanati in the freedom struggle.
64. Sri K.Bala Ghangadhara Tilak Reddy, Farmer, Business, Dokiparru - The role of Pakanati in the freedom struggle.
65. Sri Knumoori Ramireddy, Farmer, Dokiparru - Pakanati culture and customs.
66. Sri Marrivada SatyakanthReddy, IT Manager, Hyderabad - Pakanati Culture and Customs.
67. Sri Ramireddy Vinay Kumar Reddy, Indian Army, Air Force Wing, Srinagar - Pakanati Culture and customs.
68. Sri Vatrapu SrinivasaKalyanReddy, IT Manager, Hyderabad - Pakanaati villages
69. Sri Polavarapu Prabhakar,Retired, ITI College Vice Principal,Visakapatnam - Polavarapu RamaRao
70. Sri Nummagadda BhanuPrasad, Business, Vijayawada - The role of Pakanati in the freedom struggle.
71. Sri Knumoori GopiReddy, Government Printing Press, Vijayawada - Pakanaati villages
72. Sri Puritipaati NagiReddy, Farmer, Dokiparru - The role of Pakanati in the freedom struggle.
73. Sri Manda KajiReddy, Farmer, Kaza - The role of Pakanati in the freedom struggle.
74. Puritipaati SatyanarayanaReddy,Farmer,Dokiparru - Pakanaati villages

75. Sri Polavarapu UmaMaheswaRao,Farmer,Business,Visakapatnam - Pakanaati villages
76. Sri Mandali BuddaPrasad, Former M.L.A., Former Minister, Former Deputy Speaker of Andhra Pradesh Assembly, Avanigadda - 18th,19th-Century Literature.
77. Sri KiranPrabha, Kaumudi Founder & Editor, Dublin - 18th,19th-Century Literature.
78. Sri Y.KrishnaaReddy, Retired, A.P. Labour Officer, Paakanati Palle, Anantapur - Pakanati culture and customs.
79. Sri Peddinti Swamy, B.Sc Student,Jamulapalli - Pakanaati villages
80. Sri Nitin Reddy,B,Tech Student,Dokiparru - Pakanaati villages
81. Sri Peketi Chinna Kesava Reddy,Farmer,Kaza - Pakanaati villages
82. Sri Peddinti ButchiReddy, Retired Indian Airlines Officer, Hyderabad - Pakanati culture and customs.
83. Sri Peketi AdiNarayana Reddy, Farmer, Tailor, Vadali - Pakanati culture and customs.
84. Pamireddy PitchiReddy, Farmer, Dokiparru - Pakanati culture and customs.
85. Pamireddy RameshBabu, Private Employee, JangareddyGudem - Pakanati culture and customs.
86. Sri Oleti RamiReddy, Retired Irrigation Department Employee, Rajahmundry - Pakanaati villages
87. Sri Chintapalli SuryanarayanaReddy, Retired Irrigation Department Employee, Pithapuram - Pakanaati villages
88. Pamireddy NarayanaReddy, Farmer, Dokiparru - The role of Pakanati in the freedom struggle.
89. Sri Prddinti SubbiReddy, Retired Executive Engineer, Irrigation Department, Jamulapalli - Pakanaati villages
90. Sri Akkineni Bhavani Prasad, Retired N.C.C. Inspector, Farmer, Vijayawada - Polavaram Project
91. P. Mallikharjuna Rao, Librarian, Pottisriramulu University, Hyderabad - 18th,19th-Century Literature.
92. Pamireddy PratapReddy,Farmer,Dokiparru - Pakanaati villages
93. Pamireddy Satish Reddy, Private Employee, Hyderabad - Pakanaati villages
94. Pamireddy Suneela Reddy, Housewife, Hyderabad - Pakanaati villages
95. Puritipaati Sudarshan Reddy, Retired Govt.Employee,Dokiparru - Pakanaati villages
96. Polavarapu SharathBabu,Cine Director,Chennai - Pakanaati villages
97. Ramireddy VenkataReddy, Farmer, Rachuru - Pakanaati villages
98. Ramireddy RamiReddy,Suchitra Electronics,Tadepalligudem - Pakanaati village
99. Vatrapu Srinivasa Reddy, Transport Business, Hyderabad - Pakanaati villages.
100. Marrivada VenkataReddy, Farmer, Rachuru - Culture and Customs.
101. Dr.Vatrapu Lakshmi Narayana Reddy, Doctor, London - Pakanaati villages
102. Sri R. Laxman Kumar, AP High Court Lawyer, Ongole - Pakanaati villages
103. Sri Gotru NiranjanRao, Former Medak, Kadapa, Hyderabad District Collector, Director of Social Welfare Department, Principal Secretary, Finance Andhra Pradesh., Hyderabad - Pakanati culture and customs.

104. Mangina Girija, Retired RI & APGLI Officer, Hyderabad - Pakanati culture and customs.
105. Pamireddy VeeraKoteswaraReddy, Retired Hindi Teacher, kalaparru - Pakanaati villages
106. Nandula PrabhakaSastri,Author,Madanapalli - Pakanati culture and customs.
107. Dr.P.L Srinivas Reddy Ph.D., Retired Telugu Professor Anantapur - 18th,19th-Century Literature.

<u>Primary Sources</u>

01. Government Records

- Madras Legislative Council Proceedings, July 1937.
- Prison Diary, Madras, 1952.
- A.P. Legislative Assembly Debates on Irrigation-related issues.
- Madras Native-Newspapers, Police F.I.R. Reports to Home Rule, Non-Co-operation.
- Quit India Movements.
- Proceedings of the Departments of Home, Judicial, Education, etc.

02. District Gazettes

- Godavari
- Krishna
- Guntur
- Kurnool
- Kadapa
- Nellore

03. Newspapers

- A Hundred Years of the Hindu, Madras, 1978.
- Zameen Raitu, Andhra Prabha, Andhra Jyoti, Andhra Patrika.
- Bharathi, Yojana, Monthly Journals

KASTURI VIJAYAM

SUPPORTS

- PUBLISH YOUR BOOK AS YOUR OWN PUBLISHER.

- PAPERBACK & E-BOOK SELF-PUBLISHING

- SUPPORT PRINT ON-DEMAND.

- YOUR PRINTED BOOKS AVAILABLE AROUND THE WORLD.

- EASY TO MANAGE YOUR BOOK'S LOGISTICS AND TRACK YOUR REPORTING.